Repairing Pottery
and Porcelain

Repairing Pottery and Porcelain

A Practical Guide

Lesley Acton
and Paul McAuley

Lyons & Burford, Publishers

First published in the USA by Lyons & Burford, Publishers, 1996.
Originally published in Great Britain in 1996 by Herbert Press,
a division of A & C Black (Publishers) Limited, 35 Bedford Row,
London WC1R 4JH.

ISBN 1-55821-486-0

Typeset by Nene Phototypesetters, Northampton
Printed and bound in Hong Kong by
South China Printing Co. 1988 Ltd

10 9 8 7 6 5 4 3 2 1

Library of Congress Cataloging-in-Publication Data

Acton, Lesley.
    Repairing pottery and porcelain : a practical guide /
    Lesley Acton & Paul McAuley.
        p.   cm.
    Includes bibliographical references and index.
    ISBN 1-55821-486-0
    1. Pottery—Repairing.   2. Porcelain—Repairing.
    I. McAuley, Paul.   II. Title.
NK4233.A26   1996   95-48175
738.1'8—dc20   CIP

Contents

Acknowledgements

We would like to convey our sincere thanks to all those without whom this book would not have been possible:

Judith Larney and Sue Thomas for starting us on the road to conservation; Jane Evans who spent many laborious hours word-processing for us; Naomi Doctors for her artistic interpretation of our ideas; Josephine for her help and patience; Steve for his painstaking attention to the detail of the text; everybody at the Herbert Press, especially Nicky, for their help and support, and James and Lauren for having to fend for themselves while their mother was otherwise engaged in writing this book.

Introduction

Many people assume that once broken a ceramic object has
come to the end of its useful life. While this *may* be true of
purely functional wares, with a methodical approach and
the help of modern materials decorative ceramics can be
repaired. Ceramic restoration has a long history and a great
number of materials and techniques have been employed
over the years. In the past much faking took place and there
was a tendency to over-restore. Today there is much more
emphasis on honest and sympathetic repair work.

This book aims to guide the student, the amateur and
the professional restorer through each and every stage of
restoration, tackling the simple, the difficult, and the seem-
ingly impossible jobs, and to provide practical information
on every aspect of the ceramic repair process.

Ceramic repair poses many problems, from removing a
previous poor or discoloured restoration, to the challenge
of correctly dismantling, resticking and aligning shards,
and the filling and colourmatching of missing areas. All of
these are potentially difficult tasks, but by following the
guidelines and advice of this book, making trial runs and
testing materials before applying them to the object, satisfactory results can be obtained.

Weights and measures are given in metric terms, with
US and imperial versions in brackets (US pints and
gallons).

A full glossary of materials is included in the appendix
to this book. This states all relevant US alternative product
names, as well as giving a brief description of the product
and indicating its hazardous properties.

Conservation and Restoration

There is much made today of the terms 'conservation' and
'restoration' and of the distinction between them. What
exactly do these terms mean and how do they apply to

ceramic repair? *The Oxford English Dictionary* gives the following definitions:

> *Conserve:* to keep from harm or damage, to preserve especially for later use
> *Restore:* to bring back or attempt to bring back to the original state by rebuilding, repairing, repainting etc.

Thus the conservator's purpose is to stabilize an object and to prevent further deterioration, and any sensitive restoration should embrace this conservation element, as well as involving other aspects such as replacing missing parts and retouching. It must be remembered that the very nature of the material we are dealing with is inherently fragile, and that there are few pieces with any history which are not damaged in some way. The term 'repair' is used in this book to encompass both conservation and restoration.

Anyone carrying out a ceramic repair treads a fine line between doing so much work to a piece that it makes it look as though it was made yesterday, and so little that he or she fails to perform the basic duties of repair and stabilization. Whatever the balance, there are three basic rules to follow:

• Not to inflict any further damage by misuse of tools or materials or by careless handling.

• To make sure each stage is reversible, i.e. by using materials that can be removed completely and with minimum intervention.

• To preserve the integrity of the object by carrying out honest repairs without the intention to deceive.

Many old restorations are 'bodged' attempts at repair – frequently too much adhesive has been applied causing misalignment, unsuitable materials have been used in gap fills and, most commonly, overpainting has occurred in an attempt to disguise a poor repair. It is challenging to effect a complete colour match, but in conservation terms this may not always be the best solution. A well executed fill in a shade close to the body colour, which is then left as it is, is preferable to a poor attempt at colour matching, or, worse, overpainting on top of the original material. Although in some cases the owner may demand an invisible repair, the more honest approach is preferable and avoids any criticism of over-restoration.

One question which occupies many people is whether the restoration of an object detracts from its value. While it is true that over-restoration can certainly reduce the value of an object, there is no doubt that sympathetic work can at the very least make it more aesthetically pleasing.

Notes on the care of repaired ceramics

• Repaired ceramics should no longer be considered suitable for any further use except display.

• To clean a repaired ceramic use a small damp sponge, and if necessary a weak detergent solution – *do not immerse in water*. If the object is very dusty, rinse in luke warm water and pat dry with a clean tea towel or kitchen roll.

• Repaired ceramics should neither be displayed in direct sunlight nor kept in a dark cupboard.

• Do not lift any repaired ceramic by its handle; always lift with both hands, using one hand to support the base.

1 Tools and materials

There are certain items which are fundamental to the restorer's needs. It is wise to buy materials only as you need them, thus avoiding both the expense of an initial outlay and also the risk of buying expensive pieces of equipment and materials which you may find you are unable to use.

However, there are certain tools and materials which you will need to stock up on before commencing any repairs. Table 1 (p. 14) lists the basic, intermediate, advanced and specialist kits needed to carry out competent repairs safely and efficiently. By acquiring tools and materials according to these categories you may gradually build up a comprehensive range.

Support methods

Various items can be used to support objects while the adhesive is curing (drying) or while a mould is setting. These can range from adhesive tape (preferably the gentle 'magic tape' variety) and re-usable modelling material such as Plasticine, to rubber bands and plastic clamps. For delicate objects that need to be placed on their side, a cork ring or soft bean bag (or even a bag of salt) can be used, or the ceramic can be placed in a tray filled with polystyrene (styrofoam) balls.

Health & Safety

Most jobs carry health and safety risks. The main risks to arise from this type of work are from contact with epoxy resins and solvents and inhalation of dust or paint particles.

A solvent is a liquid used to dissolve other substances. Frequently used solvents in this book are water, acetone, dichloromethane (Nitromors), white spirit and xylene. Solvents can enter the body by inhalation or by skin contact. They may cause such effects as irritation of eyes/lungs/skin, headache and nausea.

Figure 1. UK hazard symbols

Toxic
Substances which present a serious risk of acute or chronic poisoning, by inhalation, ingestion or skin absorption.

Oxidizing
Substances which give rise to highly exothermic reactions in contact with other substances, particularly flammable substances.

Flammable
Extremely flammable liquids have a flash point less than 0°C and a boiling point less than or equal to 35°C.

Highly flammable substances include:

a Those which may become hot and finally catch fire in contact with air at ambient temperature without application of energy.

b Those which may readily catch fire after brief contact with a source of ignition and which continue to burn or to be consumed after removal of the source of ignition.

c Those which are gaseous and flammable in air at normal pressure.

d Those in contact with water or damp air which evolve highly flammable gases in dangerous quantities.

e Liquids which have a flash point below 21°C.

Flammable liquids are those having a flash point equal to or greater than 21°C and less than or equal to 55°C.

Harmful
Substances which present moderate risks to health by inhalation, ingestion or skin absorption.

Irritant
Substances which are non-corrosive but are liable to cause inflammation through immediate prolonged or repeated contact with the skin or mucous membranes.

Corrosive
Substances which destroy living tissue.

Safety details relating to the individual products mentioned in this book are outlined in the Glossary of materials.

• Solvent inhalation can be avoided by adequate ventilation and/or use of extraction equipment.

• Contact dermatitis can be prevented by using latex/rubber/vinyl gloves and/or a barrier cream.

• Dust/paint inhalation can be prevented by wearing a proprietary face mask.

• Use scalpels with care, and put on and remove blades using a pair of pliers.

There is now a legal requirement for manufacturers to supply health and safety data sheets for all hazardous materials – ask your supplier to provide these and always read the instructions to find out about possible dangers (see materials glossary, pp. 97–102). In the UK, COSHH guidelines (control of substances hazardous to health) are published by HMSO (see fig. 1). In the USA, information can be obtained from the National Institute of Occupational Safety and Health, Washington DC.

Storage
Generally no special storage is required for the basic materials, but when a number of cleaning materials, adhesives and solvents are collected one has to consider the implications of having potentially hazardous, toxic and flammable materials in the work area. Certain materials such as hydrogen peroxide, which is an oxidizing agent and can lead to combustion of flammables, should be stored separately.

Disposal
Do not pour out or mix up any more of the chemicals than you are likely to need for the job in hand. This is not only wasteful, but increases the problems of disposal. Proper disposal techniques will vary according to the chemical and the locale, and you should always refer to the manufacturer's instructions for the safest method.

A place to work in
Ideally, you need a well-lit north facing room with good ventilation. You will also require a sink for washing the objects in, work benches, shelves and storage cupboards. A small trolley on wheels is also a very useful addition to keep to hand tools and materials which are used frequently. Obviously the size of the room is dependent on how much work one intends to do, and therefore how much storage space one needs. Some form of air extraction

Figure 2. Conservation studio with air extraction unit

Table 1. Repair kits

	Tools	Materials
Most basic kit	Small craft knife Small metal or plastic spatula Cocktail or lolly sticks A range of artists' brushes White ceramic tiles Magnifying glass Tweezers Fine abrasive or garnet paper Small pliers	Biological washing powder Detergent liquid Cellulose nitrate adhesive Paraloid B-72 Plaster of Paris and/or Polyfilla Artists' acrylic paints Plasticine Acetone Cotton wool and tissues Scotch magic tape Safety spectacles Disposable gloves

Intermediate kit	All the above plus:
	Swann Morton scalpel handles
	  no. 3
	Swann Morton scalpel blades,
	  e.g. 10, 10a, 11, 13, 15
	Artists' brushes, preferably
	  good quality – squirrel, sable
	  or synthetic in a variety of
	  styles
	A set of small files or rifflers
	Micro-mesh cloths and
	  polishing kit
	Solvent dispenser
		All the above plus:
		Hydrogen peroxide,
		  ammonia, industrial
		  methylated spirits, white
		  spirit/turpentine,
		Jenolite rust remover
		Instant adhesive (superglue)
		Epoxy adhesive
		Dental wax sheets
		Epoxy putty (Milliput)
		Bulking agent
		Artists' acrylic varnish – matt
		  or gloss
		Bronze powders
		Powder pigments (good
		  quality)
		Disposable pipettes
		Clingfilm

Advanced kit	Airbrush with compressed
	  air supply
	Gilder's kit
		Gilding materials – Japan
		  gold size, gold leaf

Specialist kit	Mini digital scale Daylight simulation	Poulticing materials

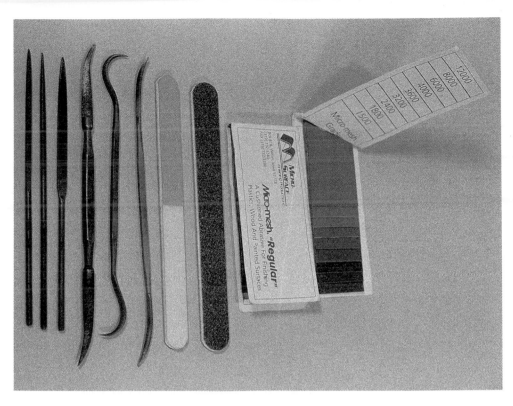

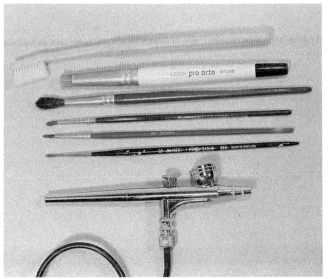

(above) Needle files, rifflers and abrasives for shaping and finishing ceramic repairs

(left) A selection of brushes and an airbrush for retouching repaired ceramics

equipment is advisable for using solvent based products or an airbrush to spray paint.

Fig. 2 shows a simple DIY air extraction unit which has been erected on the work bench. Timber supports are used as a frame, on which Perspex sheets have been overlaid and fixed into position. A small air extraction unit is placed approximately mid-way inside the unit on an outside wall. The front panel should be positioned to protect the face from any paint or solvent spray, but allowing access to the object so that it may be worked on. A small turntable is a useful addition for repositioning an object while re-touching.

Lighting

Good lighting is essential. It is important to enable you to examine the object properly, and also for each further stage, for example to allow you, once the object has been filled, to see the blemishes in the filling. Appropriate light-ing is especially vital when retouching an area, because if this is not done under the correct lighting conditions then the match of the paint may well be less than perfect, which will cause the retouched area to show. Ideal lighting con-ditions are those in which there is a north facing light and the restorer is sitting sideways on to this light. This will rarely be available and consequently artificial aids such as a daylight light bulb in an anglepoise lamp can be used close to the work. These bulbs are available from most good lighting retailers, hobby shops or conservation suppliers.

When a mixture of colours (particularly blue or a mix-ture containing blue) is viewed, the same colours may look quite different in varying lighting conditions. This vari-ation is known as 'metamerism' and is an important factor to take into consideration when retouching or making coloured fills. If at all possible work should be arranged so that colour matching takes place during that part of the day when natural daylight is at its optimum. This is particu-larly relevant during winter, when bright natural daylight may only be available for a limited period each day.

2 Examination and identification

Examining the object

The first stage of ceramic repair is to examine the object in order to identify the ceramic body and to decide how to approach the repair process. If a piece has been previously glued and (as in many cases) badly so, the object may be covered with thick brown adhesive, it may be riveted, its joints may be badly aligned or it may be completely over-painted. For all these reasons it is difficult to make a treatment plan until the object has been cleaned and you are better able to identify its needs. Sometimes you may simply be presented with a bag of pieces, in which case these should be laid out in jigsaw fashion and the examination carried out as described below.

Any examination of the object should be carried out in excellent lighting conditions and possibly with the use of a hand-held magnifying glass. You are looking, particularly at this stage, for cracks which may not easily be seen, for chips, any missing parts, and any damage to the piece which may render it unstable or which may involve extra care (e.g. running cracks).

Sometimes the piece is very dirty or it is covered in glue or has been previously restored in such a way that it is difficult to see what has to be done. In this case, you should follow the cleaning instructions given in the next chapter and clean the piece appropriately before returning to the examination. This should be done anyway on any piece that needs anything more than a simple clean.

Treatment Record

When beginning any repair it is important to start a treatment record on which all relevant information can be noted for future reference. This need not be a lengthy document, but should record the type of ware, the extent and type of damage, and the cleaning, repair and retouching methods used. It is also a good idea to photograph the object as it is received and at various stages in the repair process. An example of a completed treatment record follows.

Treatment Record

Owner's name and details: **Date:** 31·5·94

Joanne Smith, 22 The Avenue, London W2

Description of object: Small red-bodied earthenware bowl with off-white glaze and red and yellow on rim, and circular patterns (grapes) inside.

Examination

Previous repair - brown adhesive
small chip missing from rim

Dismantling

Tried warm water to remove adhesive, then acetone

Cleaning

Washed briefly in Synperonic NBD, rinsed and left to dry.

Bonding and filling

Bonded with HMG cellulose nitrate, rim chip filled with coloured Polyfilla

Retouching

Used acrylic paints in titanium white, raw umber, cadmium red, yellow ochre. Glazed with acrylic gloss varnish.

Comments

Glaze very soft, abrasive papers used with extreme care.

Identifying the ceramic body

'Ceramics' is a broad definition for all objects made from fired clay; it comes from the Greek word *keramikos* (of pottery). The term 'body' is used to describe the combination of materials that result in the three specific types of ceramic; earthenware, stoneware and porcelain. Firing these composite materials in a kiln transforms them into pottery (earthenware and stoneware) and porcelain.

The firing temperatures needed to bring about these changes are, approximately:

800–1000°C (1472–1832°F) for earthenware
1000–1200°C (1832–2192°F) for stoneware
1200–1450°C (2192–2642°F) for porcelain

Every ceramic body has a unique physical and chemical structure and yet much can be learnt by simple examination using a magnifying glass and a pen light. The handling of the body is almost as informative as observation since the feel of a surface is the best indicator of textural quality. The thickness and weight of the body are also good indicators of type. For instance, soft-paste porcelain is lighter and less dense than hard-paste. If there is a broken shard or chipped area available for examination this will be particularly useful in identifying the structure and characteristics of the body.

Low-fired earthenwares have a high proportion of impurities (lime and iron oxide). These produce a microscopically rough and 'open' texture and contribute to the porosity of these bodies – earthenwares require glazing in order to make them impervious to liquids.

Stonewares are generally off-white to brown in colour, heavy and dense. Although they will give a ringing tone when tapped this is less resonant than that given by porcelain, and totally unlike earthenware which sounds dull. Stoneware is roughly textured with a random mix of 'crystals' and some coloured impurities.

In general, higher fired wares have a glassy (vitrified), crystalline structure. Hard-paste porcelain has a dense, uniformly white, finely grained structure with a close fitting glaze. Soft-paste is similarly dense but with a more granular appearance.

Different ceramic bodies require different repair methods and materials, and accordingly it is important to know the type of body with which you are dealing. Table 2 is intended to help you identify the type of body and choose the correct materials and processes for restoration.

Figure 3. Magnified section through:

a Earthenware body; showing loose arrangement of clay particles with the glaze 'sitting' on the body

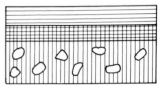

b Stoneware body; showing fewer impurities and fusion between the glaze and body

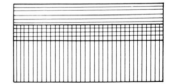

c Porcelain body; showing fine regular structure with complete fusion of body and glaze

Hints

• *Always examine the object in good light with a magnifying glass.*

• *Remember to photograph the object in its damaged state and/or draw an exploded diagram.*

19

Table 2. Identifying the ceramic body

	Earthenware	Stoneware	Porcelain
	Pottery		
Firing temperature	800–1000°C (1472–1832°F)	1000–1200°C (1832–2192°F)	1200–1450°C (2192–2642°F)
Body characteristics	Porous if not glazed Non-vitrified Clay particles loosely arranged	Partially vitrified Non-porous Coarse, granular structure	Vitrified, fine, close knit and glassy appearance Ringing note when struck with a fingernail
Typical body colour	Reddish terracotta, white, off-white, black	Beige, sandy brown, white	Usually white, if thin enough will be translucent if held up to light
Typical examples	Slipware Creamware Pearlware Tin-glaze: delftware, faience, Maiolica Unglazed terracotta Roman pottery Samian ware Staffordshire	Salt glaze Stone china Ironstone china Jasper ware Black basalts Bellarmine Caneware Cologne ware Martin ware Victorian jam jars Victorian medicine bottles	Soft-paste (most early English porcelain up to *c.*1740) Hard-paste: Chinese export wares Later Parian, Worcester, Meissen Belleek, Sèvres, Bone China
Suitable materials	**Cleaning**		
	All, but use with caution on porous bodied wares	All	All. Caution with applied decoration, e.g. gilding
	Bonding		
	Solvent-based adhesives	All adhesives, reaction-based preferable	Reaction-based adhesives, i.e. epoxy resins
	Filling		
	Plaster-based	All materials	Epoxy fills, epoxy putty, Crystacal R plaster
	Retouching		
	Acrylics	All paints	All paints

Glossary of ceramic and decorative terms

Further information relating to the identification and description of ceramic bodies is contained in this glossary.

Biscuit or bisque 'Biscuit firing' refers to a once-fired unglazed ceramic body, or the first firing of such a body. Biscuit is a semi-porous, unglazed, very white body with a chalk-like appearance. The break edge will show a granular appearance.

Body The term used to describe the characteristics of specific ceramics, e.g. colour, texture, strength.

Bone china A form of hard-paste porcelain, first made by Josiah Spode in England circa 1794. It is highly vitrified (glassy), translucent and ivory white in appearance. It is called 'bone' china because of the addition of bone ash (calcium phosphate). It is the standard English and American porcelain.

Ceramic From the Greek meaning pottery, nowadays used as a collective term to describe all fired clay products.

China clay (kaolin) An essential constituent of hard-paste porcelain.

Chinese export ware Hard-paste porcelain specifically made for export from China for European and American requirements.

Crackle A deliberate cracking of the glaze induced for decorative purposes.

Crazing An accidental cracking of the glaze, caused by differing range of expansion and contraction between the body and glaze of an object.

Earthenware Earthenwares are low-fired, opaque, porous, non-vitrified, coarse bodies.
Creamware (queensware) – cream coloured earthenware with calcined flint.
Delft – tin-glazed earthenwares from Holland.
delft – tin-glazed earthenwares from England.
Faïence – tin-glazed earthenwares from France.
Maiolica – tin-glazed earthenwares from Italy.
Majolica – Victorian version of maiolica.
Pearlware – similar to creamware.

Famille Rose (from the French name for 'pink family') – these were often bisque bodies enamelled in a highly decorative style, usually with a Chinese influence. The predominant colour of the design or ground would have been pink. *Famille* is a collective term for this type of decoration, other colours used are:
Famille jaune – yellow
Famille noire – black
Famille verte – green.

Feldspathic rock A mineral found in rocks, it is one of the most important raw materials used in ceramic manufacture.

Firing The heating of objects in a kiln. Different firing temperatures produce different degrees of hardness, porosity and vitrification.

Flux A flux can be added to clay bodies to help change the chemical properties of the clay during firing, i.e. giving greater strength and reducing porosity. Flux as a constituent of a glaze helps to reduce the melting point of the materials used in the glaze, thus allowing firing at a lower temperature.

Frit Vitreous materials used in the manufacture of soft-paste porcelain.

Glaze This is the coating applied to a ceramic body. Glazes serve both as practical and decorative finishes. The practical purpose is to reduce porosity, especially in the case of earthenwares.

In-glaze decoration – method of decoration onto an unfired but glazed surface. This causes the decoration to fuse with the glaze during firing. Maiolica and Delftware are examples of this.

Lead glaze – fired at a low temperature, transparent glaze. Common since the Middle Ages in Europe.

Over-glaze decoration (on-glaze decoration/enamelling) – coloured pigments mixed with a flux are used for decorating onto previously fired glazed wares; on refiring the pigments fuse with the glaze.

Tin glaze – a lead glaze to which tin oxide has been added. The addition of tin oxide makes the glaze opaque.

Under-glaze decoration – method of decorating the biscuit ware before glazing. The decoration is then covered with a transparent glaze and fired.

Ground Background colour of the surface of an object.

Imari Japanese wares made specifically for export to Europe. These are heavily decorated enamel wares that were much copied by many English factories in the late eighteenth century. Produced by Worcester, Chelsea and Spode amongst others.

Impasto Decorative raised glazed patterns.

Kaolin See China clay.

Opaque A body that does not allow the transmission of light.

Parian Parian is a vitrified form of biscuit porcelain. Most often found in an unglazed form, early Parian is soft-paste, with a silky texture and a slightly translucent, creamy-white body capable of showing the most intricate detail. Later Parian is of the hard-paste variety, which was easier to fire but gave a coarse-textured product that did not show the fine detail of earlier Parian. Used extensively for busts and figurines, the production of Parian ceased in the 1890s.

Porcelain The word porcelain is derived from the Portuguese word for a cowrie shell, *porcellana*. In 1516 the Portuguese explorer Odoardo Barbosa reported that the Chinese used ground-up shell in the manufacture of their translucent wares. China had a tradition of pottery making going back to 1500 BC and the first 'true porcelains' were manufactured in China in AD 618–907 during the Tang dynasty (and are known as Tang ware). The type of porcelain familiar in the West was first manufactured in China during the Yuan dynasty circa AD 1297–1368. There are two main types of porcelain: soft-paste and hard-paste. While their ingredients differ slightly, the terms 'hard' and 'soft' refer chiefly to the different firing temperatures.

Soft-paste ('artificial' porcelain). Semi-vitrified body fired at around 1200°C (2192°F). It was an attempt by the Europeans to imitate the Chinese porcelain that led to the development of soft-paste (or 'artificial') porcelain which was originally ground glass mixed with white clay. Produced in quantity by the Saint Cloud factory near Paris in the seventeenth century, it is no longer made today. Soft-paste porcelain shows a granular body when chipped. It had to be fired in an unglazed state and then refired at lower (softer) temperatures after glazing. Further firings at low temperatures were also necessary to fix the over-glaze enamel decoration and gilding.

Hard-paste ('true' or 'high-fired' porcelain). This is a highly vitrified form of porcelain that is fired at around 1450°C (2642°F). It gives a ringing tone when tapped, and shows a flint-like fracture when broken. The body and glaze are usually fired in one operation and consequently fuse together. Hard-paste is the standard European porcelain and was first made in China and much later at most of the continental factories, particularly the Meissen factory in France in the eighteenth century. The body consists of a mixture of kaolin (china clay) and petunse (a feldspathic rock). Hard-paste porcelain was first manufactured in Britain in Plymouth (1768–70) and Bristol (1770–81), but the more common British and American body is the related bone china (see separate entry, above).

Samian Ware (Red gloss pottery). Roman pottery with a smooth, shiny surface.

Sgraffito Simple form of decorating slipwares by incising a pattern through the slip to reveal the colour underneath.

Slip Slip is clay and water mixed to a creamy consistency, used for decoration (slipware) and casting (slip casting).

Slipwares Earthenwares decorated with slip. Designs were then painted, trailed, or combed on.

Stoneware These wares are very hard, vitreous and opaque. A much more durable body than earthenware.

Bellarmine is the English name given to salt-glazed stoneware wine bottles that are characterized by a bearded face on the neck of the bottle. Originally made in the sixteenth century in Germany and copied by John Dwight in England. Also known as greybeards, Cologne ware and Rhenish stoneware.

Black basalt Made by Josiah Wedgwood in the mid eighteenth century. Its body is stained with oxides of iron and manganese to produce a black vitreous ware that is unglazed though often decorated in gold lustre. Wedgwood used this for his neoclassical designs.

Caneware Also known as bamboo ware, this is a stoneware that was introduced by Wedgwood in the eighteenth century. Pieces were made to look like bamboo canes.

Cologne ware Stonewares produced between the fifteenth and seventeenth centuries in Cologne.

Ironstone is a very strong white stoneware that was used for tablewares. Originally made by C. J. Mason in the early nineteenth century, it is sometimes known as Mason's ironstone.

Jasper ware, a very fine stoneware body, cobalt blue being the most common body colour. Usually found with applied white relief decoration.

Martin ware, a decorative nineteenth-century salt-glazed stoneware, made by the Martin brothers in London and Southall.

Salt glaze, a process whereby common salt is added to the kiln during firing, producing a characteristic 'orange peel' appearance of the glaze.

Vitreous From the Latin *vitreus* for 'glassy'; applied to ceramic bodies which have a very low porosity due to vitrification caused either by high firing or by the presence of glass particles in the body mix.

3 Cleaning

The cleaning of any ceramic object should commence only after the initial examination. Investigations and spot tests can then be carried out (i.e. a cotton swab wetted with a small amount of the cleaning solution applied to an inconspicuous area) to establish which cleaning methods and materials should be employed. The cleaning process may involve the removal of loosely attached surface dirt, or greasy or waxy accretions, or the complete dismantling of previous repairs – such as old adhesive or overpainting. Other stains may have penetrated the body of the ceramic, such as organic matter like gravy, tea or oil, which may have to be removed with a soaking or poulticing process. Inorganic stains such as rust and earth may require more complex cleaning agents.

Cleaning tests should be undertaken methodically and results noted carefully. The basic approach is to employ the gentle cleaning agents before moving onto more aggressive substances, in accordance with the list shown below, until an effective method is found.

If you decide that the cleaning procedure you are using is not effective it is necessary to remove any material residue from the ceramic body before embarking on another cleaning process. This applies to all cleaning situations and materials.

Cleaning agents and processes

1 Distilled or deionized water.
2 Non-ionic detergent solution (Synperonic NBD in water).
3 Biological washing powder (either a solution of a water softener such as Calgon, and Biotex, or any biological powder, e.g. Ariel).
4 Hydrogen peroxide (20 volume) with ammonia solution.
5 Poultices – Laponite, sepiolite, fuller's earth.
6 Solvents – Acetone, industrial methylated spirits, white spirit.

Numbers 1 and 2 are mostly suitable for general cleaning purposes and can be used with soft brushes. Numbers 3, 4 and 5 are used for stain removal, particularly ingrained organic staining. Number 6 – these are usually used for degreasing and more particularly for removal of old adhesives, infills and overpainting – *use with caution!* In addition to these products, a dichloromethane paint stripper such as Nitromors can be used to dismantle previous restorations although it is not a cleaning agent as such.

Few of the materials used for ceramic restoration have been designed specifically for conservation purposes and it must be stressed that no long-term studies have been carried out as to the effects of certain chemicals on ceramic bodies and glazes. Accordingly it is not completely understood what damage may arise from cleaning agents and other material residues left in the ceramic body. However, it is known that hydrogen peroxide residue incompletely rinsed from objects causes a yellowing of porous ceramics, and has a deleterious effect on certain adhesives. Some constituents of biological washing powders, for example EDTA (ethylene diamine tetra-acetic acid) and Calgon (a water softener), may react with iron compounds in earthenware and cause discoloration, and these should therefore be used with caution. The use of chlorine-based bleaches (household bleach) can cause severe damage to the object and should not be used. Abrasive pastes and cleaners should never be used, since they can easily scratch glazes and remove gilding. Porous earthenwares should in general be approached with caution. Sometimes clay figurines are unfired and *will dissolve completely if immersed*!

Always do spot tests before proceeding.

Distilled and deionized water
This is preferable to tap water, and can be used safely with a swab or soft brush for gentle removal of surface dirt and dust. Use absorbent tissue to mop up the excess.

Non-ionic detergent solution
Use Synperonic NBD in solution with distilled water, in proportions of one drop of detergent to 50 ml water (i.e. 1:200). It can then be applied by a swab (roll some cotton wool around a cocktail stick) to clean the ceramic body. For high-fired wares this can be diluted by the addition of up to 50% of white spirit and the resultant solution shaken to form an emulsion which can then be used as a degreasing

(opposite) Removing a stain
from an earthenware bowl
using swabs soaked in
hydrogen peroxide

agent. This emulsion can be used for wet washing, but complete immersion is not recommended.

Biological washing powders

Cleaning Presoak all ceramics in clean cold water before starting any cleaning using washing powder. A solution made with a tablespoon each of Calgon and Biotex in about 5 litres (approx. 1⅓ gallons) of water can be used to immerse ceramics (complete or broken) with organic stains (tea, coffee, gravy, wine, oil) which should then be left to soak for up to twelve hours. Monitor progress carefully every twenty minutes for the first hour or two, then every couple of hours thereafter, checking that there are no adverse reactions. The solution should be changed as required and the pieces washed in clean, gently running warm water when renewing the detergent solution. Take care when leaving ceramics in running water to avoid further damage. It is not necessary to use hot water as modern enzyme detergents are capable of working at temperatures as low as 10°C (50°F), and enzymes may become inactive at temperatures above 40°C (104°F).

A more concentrated solution, consisting of one tablespoon each of Calgon and Biotex (or Ariel on its own) in a litre (2 pt) of warm water can be applied on cotton wool to an area of staining – on the bottom of a gravy boat for example – and the progress monitored. Rubbing gently with a soft toothbrush or stencil brush may assist here.

Rinsing procedure When the pieces have been cleaned to a satisfactory state, they should then be left to soak for a few days in frequently changed clean (if possible, deionized/distilled) cold water to make sure all traces of washing powder are removed.

Drying procedure After rinsing thoroughly place the object on an absorbent surface, e.g. a clean dish towel, blotting paper or kitchen roll. Leave it in a warm room for up to a week to allow the object to dry out completely. Cover with absorbent material to prevent dust sticking to it.

If the biological powder process is not working and you decide to switch to hydrogen peroxide it will be necessary to follow the prescribed rinsing procedure described above before any change of cleaning materials can be made. *Never mix cleaning processes.*

Note: while vitrified bodies (porcelain) may dry in one or two days, porous bodies are best left for up to a month to dry out completely.

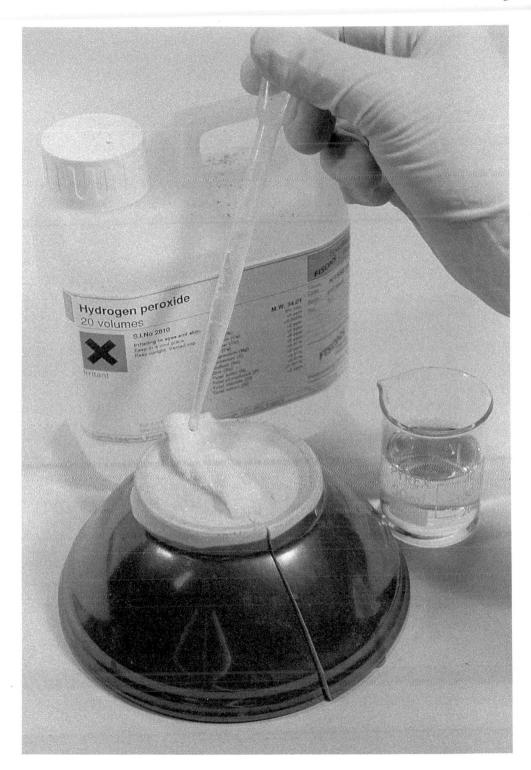

Hydrogen peroxide
(20 volume) Use this with one or two drops of ammonia (.880) solution. The ammonia solution acts as a catalyst, i.e. it speeds up the action of the hydrogen peroxide. This cleaning agent may not be suitable for use on white earthenwares because it may cause discoloration of the body. The peroxide must *never* be applied directly to a dry piece as this will only fix the stain permanently by drawing it into the ceramic body.

Soak the object for two hours in cold water and apply the peroxide solution on cotton wool swabs. Wrap in clingfilm, apply more solution with a pipette or dropper to the swabs frequently and make sure that the swabs are not allowed to dry out. When the stains have been removed soak in several changes of clean cold water and dry thoroughly as previously described.

If the stains seem to be particularly stubborn the strength of the peroxide solution may be increased by using a greater volume of peroxide to a lesser volume of water. In extreme cases stoneware and porcelain can be soaked in an undiluted solution but great care should be taken and the process monitored closely.

Poultice methods of cleaning
These involve using a material which draws out stains from the ceramic body as it dries.

Laponite is a synthetic clay which is used as a poulticing agent to remove grease and stains from various materials including ceramics. The object must be presoaked in cold water for about two hours before applying the Laponite. The Laponite is mixed with water in a 5% solution (this is approximately 2 tablespoons to 1 litre – approx. 2 pt – of water), and allowed to stand for about two hours, during which time the solution becomes a thick gel. Care must be taken during mixing to prevent the formation of lumps in the gel. The standing time may be reduced by using warm water.

The gel is then spread over the stained area to a thickness of 3 – 4 mm (approx. 1/8 in.), and the object covered loosely with clingfilm and allowed to stand. The clingfilm prevents the Laponite from drying out too quickly, which is important since the substance works by drawing the stain out gradually during the drying out process. After two to three days the cling film can be removed and the Laponite allowed to dry until it is firm but not hard (up to another three days). The poultice should then be removed and the object washed. This process may need to be re-peated several times until the object has been satisfactorily cleaned. In the case of an object with a crazed glaze the Laponite should be applied over the whole object to prevent uneven cleaning.

When dealing with organic stains (e.g. on meat plates, etc.) the object can be soaked first in a detergent solution, rinsed, and soaked in cold water before applying the Laponite. A small quantity of white spirit or industrial methylated spirit may be added to the Laponite gel to make the treatment more effective. Alternatively a small quantity of hydrogen peroxide (30 volume) and ammonia can be added to assist the removal of oily, organic stains.

Fullers earth and sepiolite These are used in exactly the same way as Laponite, although they form a paste rather than a gel when mixed with water.

Blotting paper can also be 'pulped' with a small amount of water in a food blender, and used effectively and more cheaply as a poulticing agent using exactly the same method as above.

Solvents

These are generally used to soften previous restoration materials before removal, and to degrease break edges prior to rebonding. See section on dismantling previous restorations.

Metal stain removal

Rivets and metal dowels as well as any corroded metal that comes into contact with a ceramic body may cause inorganic staining. These stains cannot be removed with detergents or oxidizing agents such as hydrogen peroxide, but require the use of rust converters. One such product is Jenolite, a form of phosphoric acid that works by converting the rust (iron oxide) to iron phosphate which can then be more easily removed from the object.

Jenolite gel should be applied to the metal stain and left for fifteen to twenty minutes, after which time it can be washed off and applied again until an acceptable level of cleaning has been achieved. As with all cleaning procedures, progress should be monitored closely. After this, follow the prescribed rinsing and drying procedure, ensuring that all traces of the Jenolite are completely removed. Any Jenolite residue left on the object can affect the setting of epoxy resin adhesive.

Steam cleaning

Steam cleaning can be used most effectively to remove surface dirt, as well as dirt ingrained in cracks. A steam cleaning unit is particularly useful for soft-bodied wares, especially those unsuitable for immersion (however this does *not* mean that it is safe to use on unfired decoration). It can reduce considerably the drying time for soft-bodied wares as well as avoiding some of the other problems associated with cleaning these wares.

Most units consist of a trigger-operated nozzle connected to a small steam generating unit. The water content of the steam can usually be controlled by a separate valve. Dirty water must be wiped away as it is produced, using

Cleaning a Parian ware figurine with a tooth brush

a clean absorbent swab. Steam cleaning units are an efficient and quick way of cleaning, the only disadvantage at present being the cost.

Dry cleaning

For some ceramics which are not suitable for wetting it may be possible to remove surface dirt with a material called 'draught clean powder' (pulverized soya bean fibre with calcium hydroxide). This is gently rubbed over the surface with a brush or soft, lint-free cloth.

A putty eraser (available from art shops) may also be used to gently rub off dirty marks if they are not completely ingrained in the porous ceramic.

Note: do not use dry cleaning methods on friable surfaces!

Dismantling previous restorations

Adhesives

All organic and animal-based glues can usually be removed with warm or hot water. Start by using a wetted swab and apply to the affected area, which should establish if the adhesive is removable with water. If after several minutes the glue is beginning to break down then the piece can be immersed in hand-hot water (provided the object is suitable for immersion) to soften the old adhesive. However, if after several minutes the glue does not appear to be softening it is possible that the adhesive is a synthetic one.

Synthetic adhesives (not epoxies) can often be broken down with acetone, methylated spirits, or white spirit. Using a swab wetted with one of these solvents should establish whether the adhesive is soluble. The solvent can then be applied onto long cotton wool rolls about 1 cm (½ in.) in diameter and laid along the old adhesive break edge. The object can be covered with clingfilm to slow down the rate of evaporation.

After application of the solvent the object may still need some very gentle pressure to dismantle the shards. If you have difficulty in doing this or the glue shows no sign of softening, repeat the process until the glue is sufficiently soft for easy dismantling.

If the solvent procedure is not working, wash the object and dry thoroughly. Using a suitable small brush apply water-based Nitromors to the old adhesive and break line; then cover the whole object or area with clingfilm which will support the object and prevent complete collapse

Figure 4

a Right angle rivet

b Acute angle rivet. Rivets imbedded at this angle will often need to be cut through before removal.

of the pieces. Monitor the process periodically. When satisfied that the adhesive is softening and breaking down, remove clingfilm and wipe off excess with disposable kitchen towel wearing heavy duty domestic rubber gloves. Then place the object in a plastic basin containing warm water. *Follow the procedure in a very well ventilated area, or preferably in an extraction booth since fumes given off can cause respiratory problems.*

If some traces of old adhesive remain on the break edges, remove with further applications of Nitromors or pick clean using a scalpel or metal point and by gently scrubbing with an old toothbrush or stencil brush. Use a combination of these tools and methods to remove *all* trace of adhesive.

When all the old adhesive has been removed wash in several changes of clean water and leave in a warm place on absorbent material (tea towel), properly supported (on a tray or plastic container) and protected from dust. When dry examine edges carefully in a side light – any old adhesive will catch the light.

Rivets

For many years the preferred method of mending ceramics was by riveting, i.e. joining the shards together by using wire staples that were fixed into holes drilled into the ceramic. Riveting, properly done, was a very skilled craft, however it is not one that should be used today because of the irreversible damage that is caused to the ceramic by the need to drill holes all over it.

It may not always be necessary (or desirable) to remove metal repairs. It may for instance be decided that they are an intrinsic part of the object's history and that they should be left in place. However, where they have become unstable or are causing staining to the ceramic body it is usually desirable to remove them. Great care must be taken not to cause further damage to the object during removal of the rivets.

Figure 5

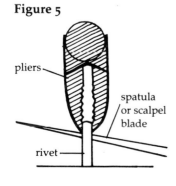

pliers

spatula or scalpel blade

rivet

When a decision has been taken to remove metal repairs on ceramics it is necessary to assess how the repair was originally carried out, to enable removal without damage to the body. Right angle rivets are usually easier to remove than acute angle rivets. The ends of the metal rivet are usually embedded in a plaster-filled hole. The plaster can be softened by applying a wet cotton swab and then carefully removed with the tip of a scalpel blade (number 11), dental probe, or fine metal point (*wear goggles*). This should

Figure 6
Chinese hard-paste porcelain
pot previously repaired with
rivets. (See case study for complete procedure.)

Figure 7

Rivet sawn in half

Figure 8

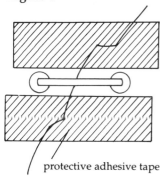

protective adhesive tape

facilitate the removal of the rivets, particularly right angle rivets. The end of a spatula can then be gently eased under the rivet which is prized up carefully, or a small pair of blunt nosed pliers or forceps can be used to pull it out (see fig. 5).

Occasionally metal rivets are lead-soldered onto the ceramic. In this case a soldering iron should be carefully employed to soften the solder, enabling the rivet to be removed.

To remove other metal wire repairs such as 'lacing' it may be necessary to cut through the wire and tease out the metal ties with a small pair of pliers or forceps. It may not be possible to cut through some iron repairs with pliers, and therefore when absolutely necessary a fine small hacksaw blade may be employed. This method may often be necessary when removing acute angle rivets as well.

Mask off the surrounding area on either side of the rivet with masking tape to prevent damage to the ceramic, and proceed with great caution. Use the hacksaw blade *with extreme caution* to saw through the middle of the rivet and remove each half separately.

Judiciously placed small pieces of adhesive tape will hold the pieces of the object together, and prevent them falling apart when the rivets are removed. The tape also helps to protect the surface of the object when using a hacksaw blade (fig. 8).

Hints

• *Only immerse non-porous wares that are stable and non-fragile.*

• *Clean all soft-bodied wares separately to avoid cross-contamination.*

• *Pre-soak in (preferably) deionized cold water to prevent stains being drawn into the body, but never allow the object to soak in dirty solutions.*

• *Take care when ceramics are being rinsed.*

• *Note that large, soft-bodied wares may take a month or more to dry completely.*

• *Remember that the final appearance of any cleaned object is often not apparent until complete drying has taken place.*

• *Crazed or weathered glazes are more at risk during the cleaning process, and on-glaze decoration is more vulnerable than under-glaze decoration.*

4 Bonding

Many diverse materials have been used in the past to repair broken ceramics. These include precious metals such as gold, used in ancient times to stick shards together and fill gaps, to later riveted repairs using lead, iron and copper rivets or 'staples'. This type of repair has been used extensively, and although aesthetically disfiguring, ethically any particularly well executed repairs should be retained as long as they are stable and not causing damage or staining to the ceramic body.

Adhesives have a long history. The earliest repairs used sticky organic matter, including such materials as gelatin, isinglass, egg, cheese and other animal products. One such material which was once in common usage is shellac, a sticky resin excreted by insects. Dissolved in alcohol, it was used as an adhesive, and is now seldom used for this purpose. However, it may be employed as a surface coating on plaster fills. Unbleached shellac is usually brownish in colour and may cause staining to the ceramic body.

Cellulose nitrate adhesives (popularly known as HMG, balsa wood glue or airfix kit adhesive) have been in use since the last century, and continue to be used widely in ceramic repair, partly due to the ease with which they may be removed. They dry by evaporation of solvent, so that adding a solvent to the dry adhesive will 'undo' the glue. Acetone is usually used for this purpose.

Paraloid B-72 is another adhesive which works by solvent evaporation, specially developed for the conservation profession. This is an acrylic polymer (polyethylmethacrylate) which is durable and non-yellowing. It is available in granular form, although for ceramic work it is much easier to use in tube form.

Polyvinyl Acetate (PVA – Vinamul, Evo-stick wood glue) are useful adhesives for the repair of earthenwares. PVAs are water-based glues.

Epoxy adhesives – other modern adhesives include a wide range of epoxy resins which although technically irreversible are widely used for high-fired wares. Common brands include Araldite, Devcon, and UHU 300+. Recently some have been developed specifically for use on porcelain and glass – HXTAL NYL-1 and Fynebond.

Instant glues (cynoacrylates), although marketed as an instant cure-all, have caused many problems due to their misuse. They do have their uses in the 'dry stick' method for tacking shards together, and for holding small shards in place (see pp. 40–42), but it is not advisable to use fast setting adhesives until you are conversant with sticking order, alignment of shards, and the general methodology of ceramic repair. A lot of damage may be caused by the unwitting use of such adhesives.

Adhesive selection

After identifying and cleaning the piece the next stage in the repair process is bonding. Before this can actually be done the correct adhesive must be selected, and you will need to consider the following criteria when making your choice.

1. Suitability/compatibility The adhesive chosen should be compatible with the type of ceramic. In general those which dry by solvent evaporation are suitable for more porous bodies (e.g. earthenwares), whilst for less porous bodies (e.g. porcelain) an epoxy resin, which sets by chemical reaction, should be chosen.

2. Reversibility Any adhesive should be removable without causing damage to the object. While this situation is an ideal, in practice it is often difficult to achieve. Adhesives such as cellulose nitrate and Paraloid B-72 dry by evaporation of solvent, and this process can be reversed using that same solvent (usually acetone). Epoxy resins set by chemical reaction and although theoretically irreversible can in practice be softened with an epoxy resin disintegrator (Nitromors) before complete removal with scalpel and a stiff brush.

3. Physical properties

a *Colour* – the *ideal* adhesive will be water-white, i.e. clear and colourless, and fortunately most adhesives mentioned in the text fall into this category.

b *Viscosity* – the extent to which a liquid resists flow. A high viscosity adhesive is thick and does not run easily; this is more suitable for an edge-to-edge stick. Low viscosity adhesives flow freely and are more suitable for dry stick repairs. It is possible to dilute some adhesives with solvent to make them flow more easily, for example acetone will dilute cellulose nitrate and Paraloid B-72, which can then be used to flow into break edges or run into cracks on earthenwares.

c *Setting time* – adhesives fall roughly into two categories: the quick setting and the slow setting. By using a quick setting adhesive (but not an instant glue) it is possible to hold the pieces together until the glue is set. This is not possible using a slow setting adhesive and some way must be found to keep the pieces together until the glue is set. This is usually done by using sticky tape, rubber bands or clamps. However, it should be remembered that some surface decoration (e.g. gilding) can be damaged by sticky tape.

d *Strength and durability* – these are usually not a problem with modern adhesives, which tend if anything to be *too* strong and long-lasting.

e *Toxicity* – handling epoxy resins can sometimes cause contact dermatitis (skin sensitivity) so that disposable gloves may be advisable. Eyes can also be affected, and accordingly great care should be taken to avoid hand/eye contact. Avoid breathing in resin dust when rubbing down fillings etc. because this may cause respiratory irritation; use a dust mask.

Most adhesives are not overly toxic but care must always be taken when handling any product of this type.

Always read labels and follow manufacturer's instructions carefully.

4. **Ease of handling and mixing** Some adhesives can be squeezed directly from the tube onto a palette without mixing. Others need to be pre-mixed by squeezing an equal quantity of adhesive and hardener onto a mixing pad, white ceramic or melinex-covered tile or artists' palette, and blending thoroughly. Others (e.g. HXTAL NYL-1) must be weighed out using an accurate scale that weighs in very small gradations. It is never advisable to apply adhesive straight from the tube.

5. **Availability and cost** Some adhesives are readily available from hardware, DIY, or artists' supply shops. Most of these are reasonably priced and easy to obtain. Other adhesives may be available only from specialist shops and may be expensive, especially if you are unable to shop in person and need to have the goods sent by mail order. However, although the initial outlay may sometimes be considerable, it is important to remember that adhesives are used sparingly, and you will only need to purchase

Table 3. The physical properties of adhesives

Product name	Colour/viscosity	Tack time/ complete set	Use as filling material
1. Cellulose Nitrate Adhesive	Clear/medium	2–3 min/24 hrs	No
2. Paraloid B-72	Clear/medium	5 min/12 hrs	No
3. Polyvinyl Acetate (Evostick wood glue)	White dries clear/ medium/high	1 hour/24 hrs	10–20% can be addedto plaster fills to strengthen
4. Devcon 5-min Epoxy	Water-white/high	5 min/30 min	No
5. Araldite Rapide	Yellow-brown – add whitening agent/high	5 min/30 min	No
6. UHU 300+ Epoxy	Yellow-brown – add whitening agent/high	90 min/24 hrs	Yes. Mix up to 30% dry material – talc, pigment
7. Araldite AY103/ HY956	Water-white/low	1 hour/24–30 hrs	Yes. Mix up to 30% dry material – talc, pigment
8. HXTAL NYL-1	Water-white/very low	3 days/7 days	Yes. Mix up to 30% dry material – talc, pigment
9. Fynebond	Water-white/very low	1 day/2 days	Yes. Mix up to 30% dry material – talc, pigment
10. Araldite 20/20	Water-white/very low	16 hrs/24 hrs	Yes. Mix up to 30% dry material – talc, pigment
11. Cyanoacrylates (superglues)	Water-white/low	instant	No

low-fired (products 1–3)

high-fired (products 4–11)

NOTE: Products 1–3 are solution adhesives which dry by evaporation of solvent

Compatibility with ceramic body	Reversibility	Mixing ratio	Health & Safety
Earthenwares	Wet – Acetone Dry – Acetone	No mixing (dilute with Acetone, if required)	Highly flammable
Good as a consolidant and for bonding all wares	Wet – Acetone Dry – Acetone	No mixing/dilute with Acetone	Highly flammable
Bonding of low-fired earthenwares and as a plasticiser for plaster fills	Wet – Acetone or water Dry – Acetone	No mixing required	
Porcelain and other high-fired wares	Wet – Acetone Dry – Nitromors	50:50	Irritant
High-fired wares	Wet – Acetone Dry – Nitromors	50:50	Irritant
Porcelain and other high-fired wares	Wet – Acetone Dry – Nitromors	50:50	Irritant
High-fired wares	Wet – Acetone Dry – Nitromors	100:20	Irritant
High-fired wares and glass	Wet – Acetone Dry – Nitromors	100:30	Irritant
High-fired wares	Wet – Acetone Dry – Nitromors	100:32.5	Irritant
High-fired wares and glass	Wet – Acetone Dry – Nitromors	100:30	Irritant
High-fired wares – use as a tacking adhesive	Wet – Acetone Dry – Nitromors or Acetone	No mixing	

products 4–11 are reaction adhesives which set by chemical reaction.

them occasionally. (See suppliers' list for details of where to purchase adhesives.)

6. Colour stability Many adhesives start off water-white, but unfortunately some may discolour in time due to the effect of ultraviolet light. Other adhesives do not start off water-white, for example UHU 300+ which is a yellow-brown colour, and in time this discoloration will become more pronounced. To counteract this a whitening agent (e.g. titanium dioxide, barytes or zinc white) should be added to the resin and blended thoroughly before the hardener is mixed in.

Table 3 summarizes the adhesives used for ceramic repair and their criteria for selection.

Consolidation

Sometimes earthenwares will have flaked or chipped edges or a friable, crumbly glazed surface. The damaged areas or break edges of these wares will need to be consolidated before any repair process can be started.

A solution of Paraloid B-72 diluted with acetone to make a 5% weight by volume (w/v) or 10% w/v solution is used for this purpose. Use the 5% solution for a small amount of damage and the 10% for areas of greater damage.

To make a 5% w/v solution: dissolve 5 g (approx. $^{1}/_{6}$ oz) of Paraloid B-72 in 95 ml (3.34 fl. oz) of acetone.

To make a 10% w/v solution: dissolve 10 g (approx. $^{1}/_{3}$ oz) of Paraloid B-72 in 90 ml (3.17 fl. oz) of acetone.

The solution is then gently painted or pipetted over the damaged area or break edges using a sable brush or small plastic pipette. More than one coat may need to be applied to very badly flaking or crumbling areas. This solution can also be used to strengthen plaster fills and any replacement parts made of plaster (e.g. handles and knobs etc.) or to seal these prior to retouching. The solution is applied in exactly the same way as described above (i.e. painted or pipetted on). In all cases allow twenty-four hours for the solution to dry.

Bonding

The two basic methods of bonding objects are the dry stick and the edge-to-edge stick. Table 4 explains which adhesives are recommended for each of these methods.

1. The dry stick method

This is a method of repair in which the shards are taped together and a low viscosity (very liquid) adhesive is

Table 4. Adhesives for edge-to-edge and dry sticking

	Edge-to-Edge	Dry Stick
Earthenwares	cellulose nitrate Paraloid B-72 polyvinyl acetate	Not recommended – glazed earthenwares only. Cellulose nitrate (diluted), Paraloid B-72 (diluted)
Stonewares	cellulose nitrate Paraloid B-72 UHU 300+ Devcon 5-min Epoxy Araldite Rapide	UHU 300+ (warmed) Araldite 20/20 HXTAL NYL-1 Fynebond
Porcelain	UHU 300+ Devcon 5-min Epoxy Araldite Rapide	Araldite 20/20 HXTAL NYL-1 Fynebond

applied in small beads along the break lines on both sides of the object. This method is mainly suitable for high-fired wares, i.e. vitreous ceramics, stoneware, porcelain and glass. It may be used with glazed earthenwares, but several applications may be necessary.

The adhesive is drawn into the break lines and spreads by capillary action, i.e. the beads of adhesive run into the cracks and are attracted to one another; this attraction causes the adhesive to spread along the cracks as each bead joins up with the next. It is very important that break edges are as close as possible together, and this can be achieved by stretching magic tape across the join. Be careful not to misalign shards when applying tape. Check by running a fingernail across.

The low viscosity adhesives such as HXTYL-NYL-1 and Araldite 20/20 etc. are the preferred options to use when dry sticking. They are specialist adhesives that have specific mixing requirements, i.e. they need to be weighed out on a fine balance or carefully measured out by volume using a small pipette.

It is possible to use thicker adhesives that do not have such particular mixing requirements (e.g. UHU 300+). Apply all along the break edges and gently warm with a hair dryer, and as the adhesive becomes less viscous it will flow between the break edges. Paraloid or cellulose nitrate may be diluted in acetone until they are sufficiently liquid

Shards of a porcelain bowl laid
out jigsaw fashion, ready for
taping

to use to dry-stick glazed earthenwares. This solution
should *not* be warmed with a hair dryer. The excess may
be removed with a slightly wetted acetone swab.

Before applying any adhesive tape check that it will not
cause damage to the surface glaze or decoration (i.e. gilding or on-glaze enamels). If it is not possible to use adhesive tape or any other support method, such as rubber
bands or clamps, then there will be no alternative other
than to use a fast setting adhesive and hold the pieces together on the work bench until the adhesive has cured.

Low viscosity epoxy resins such as Araldite 20/20
should not be used on high-fired wares that have a cracked
glaze. This will creep under the surface of the glaze adjacent to the break edges causing a 'river' mark.

Fig. 9 clarifies the following steps:

• Lay the shards out jigsaw fashion to establish the correct
sticking order, and number the pieces using labels made of
masking tape (a).

• Use magic tape to fix the shards together carefully,
stretching the tape across the joins to ensure a tight fit
(b and c).

• Apply beads of adhesive with a cocktail stick onto the
break line, at 1 cm ($^1/_2$ in.) intervals (d).

• Place the object where it will not be disturbed and cover
with clingfilm to protect it from dust while drying.

• Pare off excess adhesive with a scalpel before fully set.

• Remove tape and any further remaining adhesive.

Figure 9. Bonding a multi-break plate using the dry stick method

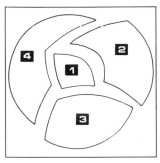 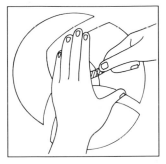 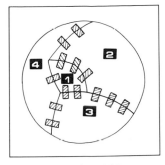

a Shards laid out jigsaw fashion and labelled in sticking order

b Shards taped together carefully

c Object ready for sticking

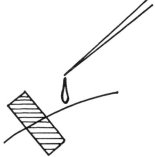

d Adhesive applied in small beads along the joins

Repairing a porcelain cup by the dry stick method

Figure 10. Using a fast setting adhesive

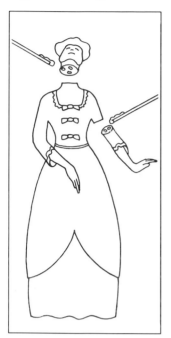

a Small dots of adhesive applied to break edge with cocktail stick

b Edges aligned and held firmly until adhesive has set

2. The edge-to-edge stick method

This is a method in which the adhesive is applied onto the break edges, and the two edges are then brought together and held firmly until the adhesive has set. This is done in one of two ways:

a By using fast setting adhesive (fig. 10).

b By using a slow setting adhesive and supporting the object, ensuring there is no movement whatsoever until the adhesive has set. Rubber bands are very useful for this purpose, but care needs to be taken that they are placed in the correct position, or the two pieces will slip apart (fig. 11). You may need several 'dry' runs to get the positioning right.

For both methods, de-grease the break edges of your object with acetone swabs, ensuring no cotton fibres are left on the ceramic.

Warning: too much adhesive will cause the misalignment of shards.

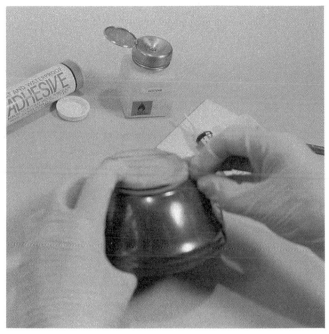

Supporting an earthenware bowl with rubber bands
after an edge-to-edge stick

Figure 11.
Using a slow setting
adhesive

Align the edges and hold in
place with rubber bands

Bonding a wedge-shaped break

Fig. 12 shows a common wedge-shaped break where
the shards of a plate are chamfered (broken at an angle).
The shards must be inserted simultaneously otherwise
they will not fit, and each shard will cause the other to be
'locked out'. Either the edge-to-edge stick or the dry stick
method are suitable for this type of repair.

Trials must be undertaken to ascertain at what angle the
break edges fit properly together, but take care during trial
runs to avoid causing further damage to the glaze at the
break edges, where it can easily chip.

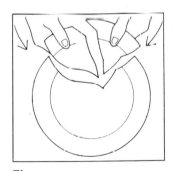

Figure 12
Shards are inserted
simultaneously for a wedge-
shaped break, either with
adhesive already applied, for
the edge-to-edge stick method,
or to be taped for a dry stick

Springing

Sometimes when an object breaks or cracks, especially if it
is curved, you may find that however hard you try the
pieces cannot be aligned, leaving a small step between the
two surfaces. This is due to the loss of tension when an
object is damaged, which causes a distortion in the shape
of the object. Sometimes it is possible to use tape or a plastic
clamp to bring the shards back into alignment. You must

13 Springing

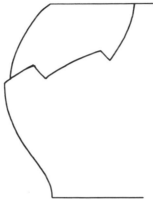

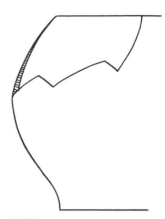

a Diagram of rebonded object showing step (exaggerated)

b Fill shaped to accommodate step and create a flush surface

however be aware that this may set up tensions in other vulnerable areas and could possibly cause more damage. If the misshapen shard cannot be satisfactorily re-aligned then the shape of the filling can be accommodated to compensate for this.

Sealing cracks

A low viscosity adhesive is useful for sealing clean cracks in high-fired wares. The adhesive should be mixed according to the manufacturer's instructions and applied along

14 Sealing cracks

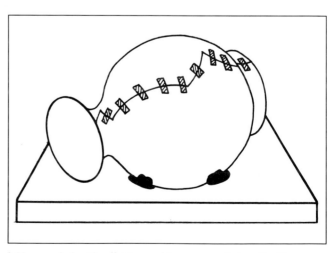

a Vase with a clean vertical crack   **b** Vase, sealed with adhesive and tape, supported on its side the crack line with a cocktail stick. Allow approximately fifteen to thirty minutes for the adhesive to penetrate the crack, after which time excess adhesive should be removed using a cotton swab dipped in acetone. Magic tape should then be applied tightly across the crack, to pull the break edges together.

Lay the object gently on its side either in a tray filled with polystyrene (styrofoam) balls or supported with Plasticine or bags of salt. Remove the tape when the adhesive has set and clean the object of any residue.

Hints

• *Always ensure you have an adequate working space so that you can sit comfortably and place the object securely on your work bench.*

• *Prepare your working area to ensure you have to hand all necessary equipment and materials, specifically clamping accessories, rubber bands, adhesive tape, mixing tile and spatulas.*

• *Before applying adhesive tape always ensure that decoration will not be damaged.*

• *Always make a trial run without adhesive. Do not apply adhesive until you have established the correct sticking order.*

• *Always select your adhesive according to the type of ware, its decoration and difficulty of repair; remember that epoxy resins should not be used on earthenwares, but may be used on stonewares.*

5 Filling, modelling and moulding

When your shards have been bonded, the next stage is to fill in any missing areas. For small areas it is usually easier to fill the gap freehand, using tape or Plasticine to support the fill until it is set. For more complicated shapes it may be possible to fill areas by taking an impression and casting missing parts with a liquid fill.

Filling earthenwares

Plaster products are the only fillers recommended for use on earthenware. Suitable types include:

Plaster of Paris
Superfine dental plaster
Crystacal R
Polyfilla
Fine Surface Polyfilla (for finishing only)

The plaster is mixed with water, which has first had a small amount of PVA adhesive (e.g. Evostick wood glue) added to it. This acts as a plasticizer, and gives added strength to the fill. Mix the plaster product with water according to the manufacturer's instructions, or about three parts plaster to one of water. Use a suitable plastic scoop or measure, and add the plaster to the water, never the other way round.

These products may be used without the addition of pigments, in which case they may need to be overpainted when dry to achieve a correct colour match. However, they can be pre-coloured by mixing with powder pigments which should be thoroughly ground and mixed in before adding to the water. All of the above products can be used in this way (except for Fine Surface Polyfilla) but Polyfilla is the most readily available. Tests should be carried out to ensure a good colour match because the mixture will become lighter in colour as it dries. To test mix a small sample of the pre-coloured plaster with water, allow to dry, and check dry sample against the object to be filled. *Remember to mix a sufficient quantity of dry coloured plaster for all the fills of the same colour, especially if a fill cannot be completed in one go.*

Mix the pre-coloured plaster to create a mixture thick enough to be pressed onto the area to be filled. Shape the fill with a spatula wetted with water, leave to dry and shape again with abrasive papers to achieve the correct profile. It can then be finished with flour paper or Micromesh finishing cloths (see p. 56). When this stage has been completed satisfactorily the fill may then be painted and glazed if necessary (see chapter 6).

It is also possible to colour plaster products with acrylic paints using the same method as above but adding the paint to the water rather than to the plaster.

Fine Surface Polyfilla is a pre-mixed plaster product that can be used to fill fine cracks and shallow gaps of less than 1–2 mm ($^1/_{16}$ in.). It can also be used as a top coat to smooth any minor blemishes in previously filled uncoloured areas. It cannot be used to fill larger areas because it shrinks slightly when set and will therefore drop out. Press the pre-mixed plaster onto the required areas using the tip of a small spatula, smooth down with the wetted tip of the spatula, and when dry abrade as necessary to achieve a fine smooth finish.

Filling stoneware and porcelain

While it is possible to use certain plaster on opaque stoneware and porcelain (for example Crystacal R), the recommended products to use are one of the various synthetic products on the market. The products listed below are the most common, but you may find others with the same properties.

1. Polyester pastes

Isopon (P38)
F.E.W. Surfacing Filler

These pastes are widely available and with care they may be used for stoneware or porcelain fills. They should be mixed according to manufacturer's instructions. However, they have limited uses for conservation purposes because:

• they are not easily reversible;

• they will not carry pigment as this will affect the curing properties;

A pearlware (earthenware) plate with moulded on-glaze enamelling

Transfer-printed English soft-paste porcelain, *c.*1820

• possible damage may be caused to the object due to the exothermic reaction when setting (i.e. they give off heat when curing although this is not usually a problem when filling smaller areas);

• they are hazardous to health.

2. Low viscosity liquid adhesives with bulking agents

Araldite 20/20
HXTAL NYL-1
Fynebond

These slower setting epoxies (described in chapter 4) can be mixed with bulking agents to create a fill that matches the translucency of the object to be repaired. The epoxy/ bulking agent mixture may further be matched with the ground colour of the object by the addition of a minute amount of powder pigment of the appropriate colours. Examples of suitable materials for use as bulking agents are:

Barytes (barium sulphate) slightly off-white

Kaolin (china clay) greyish white

Synthetic onyx powder white colour, granular texture for porcelains, especially Parian

Fumed silica (silicon dioxide), grey-white, translucent, very fine texture also used as a matting agent (i.e. to reduce gloss)

Marble dust off-white colour, usually coarse granular texture

French chalk/talc (magnesium carbonate), white to grey, fine texture

Microballons (small glass spheroids), greyish white, even granular texture.

The following powder pigments are used in these fills to make them opaque white:

Titanium White (Titanium Dioxide) brilliant white colour, use sparingly
Zinc White (Zinc Oxide) white colour

To make up the filling, first mix the chosen adhesive according to manufacturer's instructions, and ensure that the bulking agent or powder pigment is smoothly ground and free of any lumps. Gradually add small amounts of bulking agent to the adhesive, using a small flexible spatula or palette knife. A basic recipe to follow for this process is:

> 70% epoxy adhesive
> mixed with, for example:
> 20% fumed silica
> 10% talc and powdered pigment

The mixture should consist of no more than approx. 30% dry powder so as not to affect the setting properties.

Once a filling of a pliable consistency is obtained (neither too runny nor too solid; this is something that will be learnt by experience), leave the mixture to stand for five minutes to ensure all dry materials are thoroughly absorbed, then mix again. Apply to the gap, using the tip of a small flexible spatula. At this stage it may become apparent that several layers of fill are necessary, each with varying amounts of pigment, in order to achieve a good colour match. If applying several layers, allow each one to dry before applying the next, and finish with a top coat of clear epoxy if a high gloss or under-glaze finish is required. Once the filling is almost set, use a sharp scalpel to pare off any excess and abrade to a smooth finish.

3. ICI Auto Colour (Belco)

This is a cellulose stopper that may be diluted with cellulose thinners and used as a paint-on filler for very small blemishes and thread cracks. It can be lightly abraded when dry. *Use this product with caution, it contains xylene.*

4. UHU 300+ Epoxy

A suitable fill for opaque porcelains and stoneware can be achieved with UHU 300+ epoxy (or other slow setting, high viscosity epoxies) mixed with varying proportions of bulking and whitening agents.

Measure out equal quantities of UHU, mix in enough whitening agent to give a good white colour and then enough talc to make a malleable putty. The more talc added the softer the putty becomes when set, and the easier it is to rub down with abrasive papers. However, the more talc added the less sticky the filler becomes, so that one must work out a happy medium. Generally, the smaller the missing chip the stickier the filler needs to be since it has less surface area to which to adhere. To fill in a crack or chip use the edge of a scalpel or tip of a small palette knife and press the filling in. Shape and smooth with a palette knife wetted with acetone.

Hints

- *Make a small block of the filling material and keep this for later retouching trials.*

- *Be careful always to work the scalpel away from your fingers and body.*

- *For epoxy fills, use a spatula wetted with acetone to achieve a shaped and smooth fill.*

- *By stretching clingfilm tightly over the final layer of an epoxy fill it may be possible to achieve a smooth glossy finish that requires no further work.*

- *Make sure that the filling is completely smooth, as any tiny blemishes will show up once a layer of paint is applied.*

Note: slow setting epoxies such as UHU 300+ or Araldite are also suitable for use as modelling materials, when suitably bulked; add more talc than for filling.

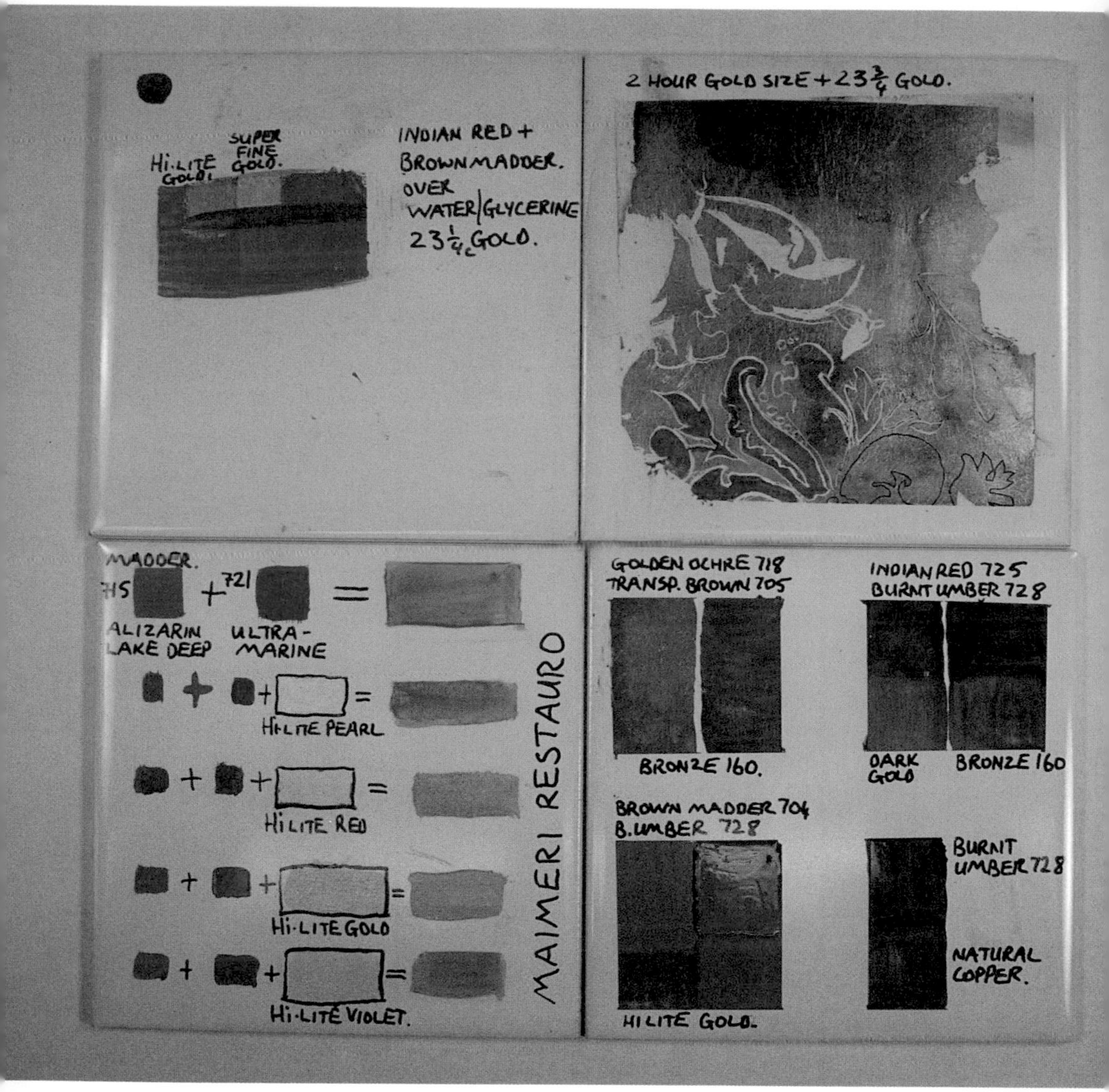

HI-LITE GOLD
SUPER FINE GOLD.
INDIAN RED + BROWN MADDER. OVER WATER/GLYCERINE 23¼ GOLD.
2 HOUR GOLD SIZE + 23¾ GOLD.
MADDER.
715 + 721 =
ALIZARIN LAKE DEEP
ULTRA-MARINE
HI-LITE PEARL
HI LITE RED
HI-LITE GOLD
HI-LITE VIOLET.
MAIMERI RESTAURO
GOLDEN OCHRE 718
TRANSP. BROWN 705
BRONZE 160.
INDIAN RED 725
BURNT UMBER 728
DARK GOLD
BRONZE 160
BROWN MADDER 704
B.UMBER 728
HI LITE GOLD.
BURNT UMBER 728
NATURAL COPPER.

Test samples of lustre pigments and gold leaf

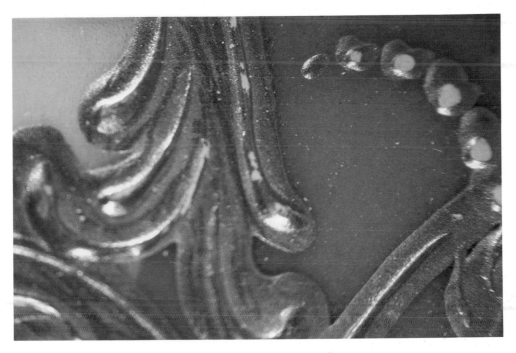

Enlarged detail of raised paste gilding on a Minton plate

Freehand modelling

Fig. 15 shows a vessel with ornate handles, one of which is damaged. The missing part can be modelled freehand, using a two-part epoxy putty. The best and most useful of the epoxy putties is Milliput, a versatile product which is available in superfine white, yellow-grey, and terracotta. Milliput has a fairly long working life and is therefore ideally suited for fine modelling work. A small amount is pressed into the area to be replaced, and will attach to the break surface without adhesive.

The two parts, putty and hardener, are simply mixed together in equal quantities, and modelled to shape *in situ*. Made slightly wet for ease of modelling, Milliput can be shaped using a variety of implements (e.g. spatulas, cocktail sticks and scalpels) and modelled as closely as possible to the same shape as the missing detail. When set, the Milliput can be further finished using a scalpel, needle files and rifflers (shaped files). Final finishing with abrasive papers and then progressively finer grades of Micromesh abrasives or flour paper should create a completely smooth surface.

Devcon Magicbond is another two-part epoxy putty that is used in the same way as Milliput. However it has a much shorter working life and sets in about an hour.

Note: two-part putties may also be used as fillers (in opaque high-fired wares only).

Micro-mesh

The Micro-mesh polishing system consists of cloth-backed cushion abrasives which are used for polishing rather than abrading. Micro-mesh regular is available in nine grades ranging from 1500 to 12000 grit. It is not necessary to work progressively through all the grades to achieve a fine finish. A selection of four to five grades should be enough to produce the correct finish, i.e. gloss, satin or matt on a coloured fill; by using the higher grades one can produce a smooth polished surface on repaired and painted areas. A small all-inclusive finishing and polishing kit can be obtained. Micro-mesh cloths are expensive but they have an extremely long life and can be washed in soap and water and re-used. A full specification is available on request from the Micro-mesh distributors' agent.

Figure 15. Freehand modelling

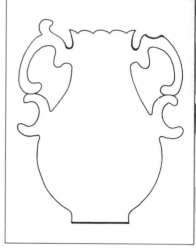

a Vessel with damaged handle

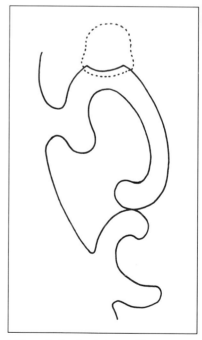

b The missing knob is roughly modelled up in Milliput

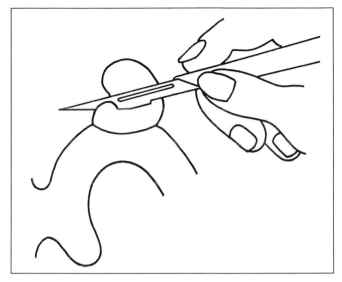

c When set it is worked into shape using: 1. Scalpel

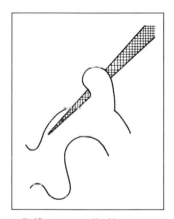

2. Rifflers or needle files

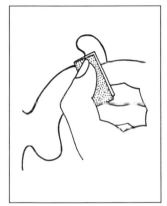

3. Abrasive/finishing papers

Hints

• *For flat shapes, modelling material may be rolled out with a rolling pin. Use talc to dust and cut to shape using a craft knife, scalpel or cake icing cutter for flower shapes.*

• *Practise freehand modelling with Plasticine or other re-usable modelling material before using an epoxy putty.*

Freehand modelling

Wedgwood jug handle modelled freehand and retouched to match original glaze

Making a two-piece mould

Extant cup handle covered with
Plasticine barrier (bottom) and
impression compound (top)

(below) In situ impression
compound coated in release
agent

Moulding

This is a process whereby a missing part can be replicated and replaced using an existing detail on the piece itself or on another similar piece (for example a cup handle). An impression is taken of the extant detail and the impression material is then filled with a liquid fill to make a cast of the required piece. When set, the cast is removed from the mould and fixed into position on the object. This is a particularly good way of replicating complicated or difficult shapes.

Where no extant detail is available the missing piece will have to be modelled freehand. Further, moulding may be expensive, and is a technically challenging process, so for the one-off piece the repairer may prefer to model freehand in any event.

Plasticine or other such re-usable modelling material can be extremely useful in the making of moulds.

Impression materials

Your choice of impression material will depend on the type of mould required to cast the replacement piece. Before using any impression material ensure it is suitable and compatible by testing if necessary on an inconspicuous area, to check that it does not stain the body or remove any surface detail. Take particular care with unglazed and low-fired wares (earthenware). If it is not possible to use any impression material because of the delicate nature of the ceramic body then the missing detail(s) will have to be made by the freehand method.

There are many impression materials available, the most common being dental wax, rubber latex, silicone rubber and silicone compounds.

1. Dental wax These pink wax sheets about 200 mm × 75 mm (8 in. × 3 in.) are very useful for simple moulds, and with some ingenuity can be applied to many projects. They are useful for achieving a correctly shaped fill on a vessel that is accessible from both the inside and outside. The wax can be softened in hot water or with a hair dryer. When soft it is pressed gently onto an existing area and allowed to harden. It can then be carefully removed, reapplied to the missing area, and filled using an appropriate filler.

2. Rubber latex and silicone rubber compounds Rubber latex is versatile and relatively inexpensive. It is applied in successive thin coats and left to dry for about ten minutes to half an hour at 20°C (68°F). About six coatings may be necessary before the final coat. This final coat consists of latex mixed with a bulking agent (e.g. talc or fine wood flour) and is used to support the thin latex layers. The impression is then removed (cutting and resealing if necessary) before being filled with an appropriate casting material. Copydex adhesive (rubber latex adhesive) can be used in the same way as rubber latex solution.

Silicone rubbers are used in the same way as rubber latex except, rather than air drying, a catalyst or accelerator is employed. A common silicone rubber product is Ambersil. Mixing amounts are critical, so refer always to manufacturer's instructions, and observe the safety note about the irritant nature of the catalyst.

Note: Both rubber compounds are useful for replicating fine detail on glazed ceramic bodies, but they should be used with caution on porous earthenware as they may stain the body.

3. Steramould This is a non-viscous silicone impression material which when mixed with a hardener may be pressed onto the detail to be replicated. When set (approx. fifteen minutes) the Steramould impression is gently prized away and filled with an appropriate casting material.

Dental wax moulding

A typical use of a dental wax mould would be for the repair of a rim chip. (Wax is not suitable for larger epoxy resin fills due to the heat generated during curing.)

Before making the mould, cut the wax sheets to size, making them approximately 1.5 cm (3/4 in.) wider than the gap to be filled.

Fig. 16 clarifies the following steps:
• Soften wax and apply to both sides of an intact edge (b).
• Remove the wax moulds from the intact edge and fix and seal onto the area to be filled, using magic tape or Plasticine. Be careful not to distort the mould or remove any surface decoration (c).

Making a two-piece mould

Newly cast handle – note indentations for matching up two halves of mould

New handle adhered to cup and ready for retouching

Figure 16.
Filling a rim chip

See photographs in case study
of small coffee cup

a Vessel with rim chip

• Coat the wax sheets with a polyvinyl alcohol release agent (PVA) or a very thin coat of vaseline to prevent the wax sticking to the casting material. Add one or two drops of washing-up liquid to the bottle of release agent to help break up the surface tension.
• Pour in liquid fill (plaster or epoxy as appropriate, see pp. 48–53) making sure it runs into all the gaps of the break edge. When filled to slightly above the rim tap gently to remove air bubbles or release them by bursting with a needle or cocktail stick (d).
• Wait until fill is completely set before removing wax sheets, remove excess fill and abrade to a suitable finish.

A similar technique can be used to fill in missing areas of body on vessels (e.g. plates, cups, bowls). In this case dental wax impressions should be taken of the body from the face side and the filling pressed in from the underside. The filling should be smoothed down using a spatula wetted in acetone for an epoxy fill, or with water for a plaster fill before the filler is completely hardened.

b Dental wax impression taken from both sides of an intact edge

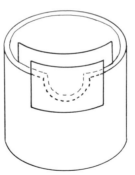

c Wax mould moved around to cover chip

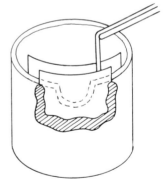

d Wax mould fixed in place with tape or Plasticine and filled

Making a mould with an impression compound
1. A one-piece mould Where it will be possible to remove the mould easily (e.g. where the detail is a simple shape with no undercuts) an impression compound can be applied over an existing detail. When the impression compound is set, it can be removed by cutting with a scalpel or scissors down the centre of the outside edge, and carefully opened and peeled away. The mould can be held

Figure 17. Making a one-piece mould

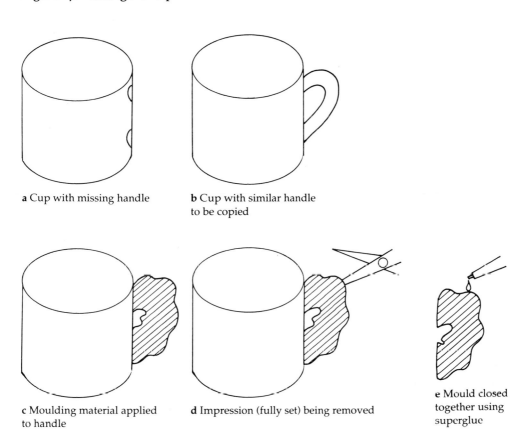

a Cup with missing handle

b Cup with similar handle to be copied

c Moulding material applied to handle

d Impression (fully set) being removed

e Mould closed together using superglue

together using superglue or closed up tightly using tape (take care not to distort the mould when closing it together), and is then filled with an appropriate casting material and left to set for as long as necessary. The resulting cast can then be gently removed from the mould and adhered directly to the break (see fig. 17).

2. **Making a two-piece mould** A further development of impression taking is where the mould is taken in two separate halves and then joined together. This method should be used where the shape is particularly complicated and/or contains many undercuts. It is also a good way of taking an impression of a delicate area, since the risk of further damage is minimized by the separate removal of each half of the impression. Fig. 18 clarifies the steps to be followed when replicating a detailed cup handle.

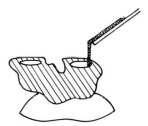

f Mould supported on Plasticine base and filled with casting material

Figure 18. Making a two-piece mould

a Double-handled cup with one handle missing

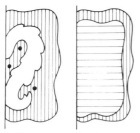

b Plasticine applied to one side of existing handle (note indentations)

c Impression compound applied over handle and Plasticine

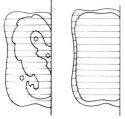

d Plasticine removed and *in situ* impression compound coated with a release agent

e More impression compound applied over open side of handle and *in situ* compound

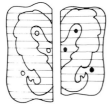

f Mould peeled off in two parts once set

• Roll out a block of Plasticine and apply over one side of the handle to be replicated. Use a pencil to press two or three indentations into the Plasticine; these will be the locating points of the two-piece mould (b).
• Press the impression compound onto the side that is not covered by the Plasticine barrier (c).
• When impression compound has set remove the Plasticine, making sure you remove all traces from the ceramic and impression compound. Leave impression compound *in situ* (d).
• Coat the inside of the *in situ* impression material with a PVA release agent or a very smooth thin coat of vaseline, to prevent the two parts from sticking to each other once further impression compound has been applied to the other side of the handle (d).
• Press more impression compound onto the exposed side of the handle (e).
• When set the mould should be peeled away from the object in two separate parts (f), and then these two parts closed tightly with tape or superglue. The location dimples will assist in the re-aligning of the two parts, which must be exact.
• Support the mould with Plasticine or on a small cork ring before pouring the casting material into the hole at the top of the handle.

Note: A mould can be made in more than two parts if the shape is very intricate or large. Plasticine can be used to fill in some undercuts if this will help to make a simpler mould.

***In-situ* casting** Sometimes it is possible to cast missing pieces directly onto the break edge (see fig. 19). This is a particularly useful method when replicating handles, knobs and other details where there is one to copy. It ensures a good or even exact join if care is taken during the process.

When set remove the mould and any Plasticine etc., then trim, abrade and finish as previously described.

Casting materials

As with all ceramic repairs materials appropriate for the ceramic body should be used. The appropriate casting materials (liquid fills) are:

For earthenwares or any other low-fired or unfired wares: plaster based products, for example:

Polyfilla, plaster of Paris, dental plaster, Crystacal R.

Figure 19. *In-situ* casting

a Object with broken handle and extant detail available for copying

b Impression of extant handle taken with suitable impression compound (make a single or multi-part piece mould as necessary)

c The mould is removed from the extant handle and two small holes are cut in it: one to allow the casting material to be poured in; the other, slightly smaller, to allow the expulsion of air.

For stonewares and porcelain (high-fired wares):

slow setting epoxy resin adhesive e.g. Araldite 20/20; for opaque wares it is possible to use UHU 300+ or Crystacal R.

Casting with plaster
When mixing plaster products always add plaster to water/PVA solution and do not stir until the powder has absorbed the water, then mix to an even consistency ensuring no air bubbles develop. Use a flexible container (rubber ones are available, or use a clean yoghourt carton) and be ready to pour the mixture when a thick liquid consistency is achieved. Squeeze the container to form a pouring lip, and pour slowly to ensure air does not get trapped, especially in the corners of the mould. If necessary burst air bubbles and release air pockets immediately using a cocktail stick or needle.

Casting with epoxy resins
The epoxy resins should be made up according to manufacturer's instructions, and can then be whitened, and/or coloured, and bulked if and as necessary, as for fillers (see pp. 52–53). When the correct opacity and colour (and possibly texture) has been obtained, the mixture should be left to stand for five to ten minutes, mixed again and then poured very slowly into the mould.

Make sure that it flows into all areas, particularly if the mould contains small sections (e.g. a mould of a small hand or foot). Tap the mould gently to allow any air bubbles to rise to the surface and prick these with a needle or cocktail stick.

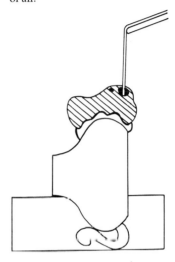

d The mould is fixed (with Plasticine or other suitable materials) onto the remains of the handle to be replicated, and the object suitably positioned (here it is propped up sideways in a small box filled with polystyrene balls and placed securely on the bench). The casting material should be poured in very slowly to avoid trapping air bubbles.

Finishing

When the liquid fill (plaster or epoxy) has fully set, remove the moulding material and trim, shape and abrade the cast as necessary. Any small air holes or gaps will need to be filled with the appropriate materials and then the whole area finished to a smooth unblemished surface with abrasive papers (and possibly Micro-mesh cloths). When this stage has been satisfactorily completed the area may then be retouched if necessary.

Table 5. A summary of filling and modelling materials

Type of material and product name	Ceramic body	Colour	Complete set at 20°C	Uses	Addition of pigment	Health & safety
ICI Auto Colour	Stoneware and porcelain	white	24 hours	Fine filling and thread cracks	no	Harmful
Polyester pastes	Stoneware and porcelain			Filling		Flammable
F.E.W.		off-white	15 mins		no	
Isopon P38		grey	15 mins		no	
Plaster products	Earthenware and stoneware			Filling/casting		Irritants
Polyfilla		off-white	1 hour		yes	
Plaster of Paris		white			yes	
Dental plaster		off-white			yes	
Crystacal R		white			yes	
Fine Surface Polyfilla		off-white		Only fine fills and cracks	no	
Epoxy adhesive fills	Stoneware and porcelain	white/ translucent	Refer to adhesive chart for individual set times	Casting and filling only	yes	Irritants
(70% adhesive, 30% bulking agents and powder pigments)						
UHU 300+ (with bulking agents and white pigment)		white		Filling, modelling and casting	whitening agent only	
Epoxy Putty	Stoneware and porcelain			Modelling (and filling)		Irritants
Milliput		various	24 hours		no	
Magicbond		off-white	1 hour		no	

6 Retouching

When the ceramic has been rebuilt and any gaps filled, the next stage, where necessary, is colour matching to replicate the surface glaze and decoration. This may take many different forms. For example, it will be fairly simple to paint on a clear coating over a well coloured fill to simulate a clear glaze, but for other pieces it may be necessary to apply several tinted coatings to achieve the correct depth of colour and opacity. There is a wide variety of different types of glazes: some may be thick and glassy, while others may be thin and translucent, sometimes the glaze may 'sit' on the clay body, while other glazes are more close fitting. Some ceramics are unglazed and matt in appearance, for example Parian and terracotta.

The retouching and colour matching of a ceramic repair is potentially the most challenging part of the repair process. There are many types of surface to simulate and a wide range of materials from which to choose, and it may be necessary to undertake many trials (and suffer many errors!) to achieve the correct colour, texture and finish.

Replicating a glaze

A binding agent is an essential ingredient for applying colour, acting as a vehicle for the pigment and holding it in place after drying. Used alone, a binding agent (which may be in the form of an adhesive or a varnish) will replicate a clear gloss or satin glaze. The addition of colour or a thinning medium (i.e. water in the case of water based acrylic media) can change the character of the glaze by, for example, making it more or less translucent, and giving a greater or lesser degree of gloss. It is vital to use a medium that does not yellow. Media which are not light-stable are of no use to the ceramic restorer.

Generally, a pigment (colour) and binding agent (carrier for the pigment) are mixed to produce a retouching medium. There is a range of binding agents available.

Some types are ready to apply, while others need to be mixed on a palette or tile with a spatula. Whichever binding agent is chosen, tests should be carried out and samples left to dry to check colour and texture. When copying any decoration, simulate the design as a trial run on a suitable surface, such as a plain white tile or the squares of set filling material previously set aside.

Adhesives

Some adhesives mentioned in the adhesive chapter can be used to simulate a glaze on a repair. The following low viscosity epoxies suit porcelain and high-fired wares:

Araldite 20/20

HXTAL NYL-1

Fynebond

These adhesives may also be used as binding agents for the application of a pigment.

Acrylic varnishes

Acrylic varnishes in gloss, satin and matt are suitable for application over acrylic paints and give satisfactory results for a number of finishes. They have the advantage over others of being solvent-free, usually water based, fairly safe and simple to use, and clean. There is at least one turpentine based acrylic varnish which is suitable for admixing with mastic bound restoration colours, such as those produced by Maimeri (see below).

Another commonly used material is Rustins Plastic Coating, which produces excellent results, particularly when applied with an airbrush, but is rather difficult to dilute sufficiently to do so. Its thinner is rather toxic and flammable and must be used with some form of extraction equipment. It can be coloured using solvent based colours, e.g. Maimeri restoration colours, ceramic and glass colours and finely ground dry pigments.

Colouring media

There is a wide range of colouring media that may suit the ceramic restorer, some of which need to be mixed with a binding agent, and some of which can be applied directly, although they can be thinned as required by mixing with a suitable solvent.

Powder pigments

Good quality powder pigments can be purchased from hobby or art shops. Only small amounts of pigment are needed for retouching and therefore small quantities will last a long time. However, the initial outlay can be expensive. They are not the easiest medium to use, but are a necessary purchase if you wish to make coloured repairs. Powder pigments are the only colouring agent to mix satisfactorily with all binding media. Some pigments are finely ground, while others may be coarse. All pigments should be thoroughly ground on a white ceramic tile with the tip of a spatula to get rid of any lumps before adding to the binding agent.

Recommended binding agents for mixing with powder pigments

Epoxies such as HXTAL NYL-1, Araldite 20/20, and Fynebond

Water based acrylics – Liquitex Gloss

Solvent based acrylics – Rowney Acrylic Soluble Gloss Varnish

Maimeri restoration colours

Available in thirty-two colours, in 20 ml (14 fl. oz) tubes, Maimeri restoration colours are pigment mixed with mastic resin binder and turpentine solvent. One of the few products specifically made for restoration purposes, they offer an excellent, if expensive, retouching medium. Drying time is approximately ten to fifteen minutes (depending on temperature). Once dry they are easily removed with turpentine. Maimeri colours dry to a matt finish so may need a final application of gloss varnish to match surrounding area or alternatively they may be mixed with a Rowney acrylic gloss varnish before application. For airbrushing pre-mix with Rowney acrylic gloss varnish and thin with turpentine if necessary.

Cold ceramic and glass colours

This is a range of inexpensive paint that is widely available from artists' supply shops. They are translucent colours which dry to a glossy finish, and can be applied by hand or airbrush. A final coat of gloss varnish may be applied if necessary. Manufactured by Lefranc and Bourgeois (as Vitrail) and Maimeri, and available from most art shops. Thin and clean with turpentine.

Acrylic paint

Acrylic paint is pigment bound in an acrylic (plastic) binding medium. Today, this paint is available in a vast range of colours and textures from a variety of manufacturers, with a particularly excellent range available from Liquitex (Liquitex high viscosity artist colour). Acrylics are probably the easiest and safest colouring medium to use, as well as being cheap and easily available. They dry rapidly which is a great advantage where there is a need for more than one application. The main disadvantage with this kind of paint is that it tends to be difficult to smooth down and polish. However, this can be overcome to an extent by abrading very gently with the finer grade Micro-mesh polishing cloths (8000 or finer).

As acrylic paint dries the water evaporates and the plastic particles join together to form a cohesive coloured film. The loss of water causes a change in the refractive index (i.e. a change in the angle of reflected light), the consequence of which is to make the paint dry to a slightly darker shade. This has to be compensated for when colour matching. The easiest way to do this is by allowing a small patch to dry on a Melinex film or ceramic tile and checking that the dried sample is the correct colour match needed to retouch the affected area.

Acrylic paints are suitable for application by hand- or airbrush; if necessary dilute with water or a specialist airbrush medium. Clean any mistakes off with water while wet, or acetone or turpentine when dry.

Some manufacturers produce excellent booklets on acrylic paints and their use. One such by Liquitex, *The handbook of fine art techniques and applications for acrylic paints, mediums and varnishes* is available on request.

Colours

Each of the colouring media just described comprises a range of colours of which those listed below are the most useful (although they sometimes can be found under alternative names). It should, however, be noted that the same pigments will perform in slightly different ways depending upon which binding agent and particular manufacturer's product is used, since different products (of the same colour) have slightly different tinting and covering properties.

Ask your stockist for a colour chart and keep to hand when working.

alizarin crimson vivid, highly transparent colour.
barytes slightly off-white.

burnt sienna coppery red, adds warmth. A transparent colour.

burnt umber a richer brown than raw umber; with stronger tinting abilities.

cadmium reds light or medium cadmium red for a bright red; dark cadmium red for a deeper coloured red. These reds are opaque with a strong tinting power. Mix with yellow to make orange. Will not mix with blue to produce purple.

cadmium yellow a strong opaque colour that is obtainable in light, medium and dark with good tinting power. Mix with blue for green and mix with red for orange.

cadmium orange a bright strong opaque orange; more yellow than red.

cerulean blue a green-blue that is weak and transparent.

cobalt blue produces cool and subdued tones; a weakish colour and tint.

lemon yellow a light cool colour with a weak tinting power; use to make vivid oranges and greens.

mars black darkest black; a strong colour; can be used to make tones.

monastral blue a vivid strong blue. It will make bright purples and greens when mixed with crimson and yellow respectively. Makes sky blue when mixed with white.

monastral green a deep and bright colour. A very strong colour with excellent tinting ability. Can be mixed with white to make pale blue-green.

pale olive green a dull brown-green with average tinting abilities.

raw umber earth brown colour; use to tone and darken other colours. Semi-transparent; has a poor tinting power.

raw sienna an opaque sandy colour; fairly good tinting strength.

red ochre rich iron-oxide rust red.

titanium white a strong tinting power; can make paler hues as well as alter a colour profoundly.

ultramarine blue a deep blue; mix with crimson to make purple. Mix with yellow to make greens. A transparent weakish colour.

ultramarine violet a deep purple with good tinting power.

yellow ochre a dark dull (earth) yellow. Semi-transparent, good tinting strength. Use with blacks and blues to give dull greens. Mix with white, burnt sienna and blue for flesh tones.

zinc white semi-opaque white.

It is considered that the following colours are the minimum necessary to produce a suitable palette of colours for retouching:

alizarin crimson	*mars black*	*titanium white*
barytes	*pale olive green*	*ultramarine*
burnt sienna	*raw umber*	*yellow ochre*
cadmium red	*red ochre*	*zinc white*
lemon yellow		

Brushes

The type of brush used for painting may also affect the quality of the final retouching. Sable or sable and synthetic blend brushes are excellent for restoration purposes. Quality brushes that have a good spring and do not shed hairs will not make you a better painter, but they may help to give a better finish. Brushes should be chosen with care and properly looked after.

Most manufacturers produce helpful and informative leaflets on choosing and caring for your brushes. Recommended is *The Art of Choosing the Right Brush*, published by Winsor & Newton and available from artists' supply shops. The most useful shapes for ceramic retouching are:

Spotter Used for fine detail. These brushes are available in very small sizes (00000) to much larger 6, 7, 8 & 9. The 0 or 1 sizes are the most practical as they can carry more paint than the smaller sizes and therefore do not dry out as quickly. The tip on a 0 or 1 should (in theory) give you as fine a stroke as the smaller sizes.

Flat This carries more paint than a spotter and is useful for lines and where a hard or angular edge is required.

Fan This gives a soft shaded effect and is also very useful for applying a top coat of varnish.

Fine Liner (rigger brush) This has a longer than normal brush head, and is excellent for painting fine lines.

Striper A brush used to draw stripes.

Airbrushes

An airbrush is a small hand-held tool that is connected to a compressed air supply. The air supply is used to propel a stream of paint onto the object to be sprayed. The advantage of an airbrush is that it can give a smooth area with no hard edges. It is invaluable for background retouching and is also extremely useful for the painting of parts that have not been made *in situ*. These objects can be sprayed and then fixed in place. The great danger with an airbrush

Hints

• *Always clean your brush immediately after use in suitable solvent then wash in soapy warm water.*

• *Brushes must be clean and dry before storing.*

• *Do not mix paint with a brush, apply colours to a tile and mix with a spatula.*

• *Do not rest on hairs.*

• *Practice with each brush to determine its applications.*

is that you may end up overspraying a much larger area than is necessary. You may also end up with paint in many places on the object where it should not be. Great care must be taken to mask off areas not intended to be sprayed. Clingfilm is suitable for this since it produces a masking medium that will not disturb any areas underneath, especially where there may be other repairs.

The independent double-action airbrush is the best choice for the ceramic restorer. This incorporates variable air–paint ratios as well as being able to be controlled by a finger operated trigger action. This type of airbrush allows for a range of applications, from the painting of fine lines through to covering larger areas of background.

Recommended airbrushes are:

Iwata
Rotring
Aero-pro

A good supplier will explain the pros and cons of each.

Using an airbrush correctly is a skill that can be mastered with patience. The easiest way to master this skill is by practising with the help and instruction of the step-by-step guide books available from your airbrush stockist or local library. Most airbrush centres are very helpful and will give advice on the use and care of your airbrush. It is also a wise precaution at the time of purchase to ensure that your airbrush centre offers servicing and spares for your equipment.

To propel the paint a source of compressed air is needed, which can be in the form of an air canister or an air compressor. An air compressor offers a better air supply, in terms of economy and keeping the air supply at a constant rate. There are mini-compressors through to slightly larger units available, depending upon individual needs. Canisters are obviously less expensive initially, although the cost of replacing empty canisters should not be underestimated. Contact your supplier to find the air supply best suited to your needs.

Replicating gilding on a ceramic repair

Gilding is the last decoration applied to fired ceramics and it should be the last when retouching a repair. With patience and care acceptable results can be accomplished – be prepared to make several trial runs. Gilding is a specialized process involving a separate range of materials, but mastering the techniques and methods provides a worthwhile challenge. Of all the materials available nothing can give quite the same excellent finish as real gold leaf itself.

The area to be gilded should be clean and completely smooth and free of any blemishes. In any retouching process, any surface irregularities will become more apparent when a finish is applied.

Match the correct colour, which may be done by blending when using gold paints or bronze powders. When using gold leaf it is not possible to blend colours and the correct match must be made from the available selection.

Gilding materials (except gold leaf)
Gold enamel paints These do not give a good finished appearance and are not recommended.
Acrylic gold paint Cheap and easily available. The range is developing; different makes will give different results and they should therefore be tested before using. Apply using a brush or airbrush.
Gold ink This consists of metallic particles suspended in a shellac medium. It can give acceptable results but usually needs more than one coat and lacks the lustre of real gold. Apply using a brush or airbrush.
Gold pens These are fairly good for retouching small areas although they often tend to develop a greyish tinge when dry. They may be applied directly from the pen if the nib is fine enough, or by pressing the nib several times onto a white ceramic tile. This will give you a small pool of liquid gold which can then be applied with a fine brush.
Gold paint and varnishes These are metal powders suspended in a liquid medium; they are easy to apply by hand with a brush or with an airbrush. They often give an acceptable finish but again these lack the lustre of real gold.
Bronze powders Bronze powders are available in a variety of colours ranging from pale gold to a deep copper colour. If necessary they may be mixed with appropriate pigments to obtain a correct colour. There are three particle sizes available. *Standard bronzes* have the largest particle size, *lining bronzes* have a smaller particle size, and *burnishing bronzes* have the smallest particle size. It is preferable to use the burnish bronze powders if they are obtainable.

As bronze powders are usually quite coarsely ground they need to be ground further. Grind the powder with the spatula tip onto a white ceramic tile. Apply in the same way as gold powder.

Gold powder (shell gold) Gold powders are more finely ground and therefore generally give better results than bronze powders, but are expensive. All powders need to be applied using a suitable medium, such as gold size or an acrylic varnish.

Match the colour to the original as closely as possible, with the addition of pigments if necessary to obtain an exact match. Maimeri restoration pigments or Lefranc and Bourgeois cold ceramic and glass colours are the most suitable media for mixing with gold powders. If these are not available then powder pigments may be used. These must be thoroughly ground so that the resulting mixture is not lumpy. When the correct colour and texture has been obtained it can then be applied with a hand-held brush. For application by airbrush it may be necessary to dilute the mixture with the appropriate thinning agent. Gold and bronze powders mixed with any medium must be stirred frequently during application, since heavy gold and bronze particles tend to sink to the bottom of a suspension.

An alternative method of applying powders is to dust the entire area with a little talc applied on a no. 7 squirrel brush. The area to be gilded is then 'painted in' using a gold size (see below) or an appropriate medium mixed with a little suitable pigment, e.g. alizarin crimson for a reddish gold and mid-chrome yellow for a yellow gold. By using a tinted size it is easier to see the actual area that has been painted. When the size is tacky the powders can be applied by soft brush, by gently sprinkling the powder from the brush over the area to be filled in. When dry, brush the excess powder off, and seal using an acrylic varnish applied with an airbrush.

Gold leaf

Gold leaf is without a doubt the best way of restoring gilding onto ceramics. It is the only medium that can replicate the original finish, and despite the initial cost and difficulty of handling, it cannot be bettered. With practice and care it should be possible to master the techniques and materials involved. Loose gold leaf and transfer gold leaf are available in books of twenty-five leaves, the only difference being that the transfer variety is backed with a sheet of tissue paper which is peeled off when the gold is transferred. Since gold leaf cannot be blended to obtain colours it must be matched correctly before application. Colour is determined by the purity of gold, and charts for matching are available from gilding suppliers. Where gold leaf will not produce an exact match, Schlag metal leaf can be used instead.

Both transfer and loose gold leaf need a medium to fix them onto the ceramic. This medium is known as gold size, and is available with various drying times; the Japan variety being the quickest drying size, with a tack time of approximately twenty minutes depending on the temperature and humidity of the working environment. Other available sizes have varying tack times of between two and sixteen hours. The slower drying sizes give better results due to the self-levelling properties being given longer to work. The longer the size takes to become tacky the better the gloss and the longer the working time you have available. Lack of working time is not, however, usually a problem when gilding onto ceramics because the working areas are generally fairly small. Also, when using a slower drying size the difficulty of keeping the object in a dust-free environment, combined with the difficulty of arranging working times, often outweighs the advantages.

Equipment Working with gold leaf is a very delicate business and requires the following specialist equipment:

A gilder's cushion which is a padded, leather-covered board with a draught screen fitted around one end.

A gilder's knife which is used to cut the gold on the cushion, alternatively a butter knife with a straight, smooth blade can be used, which should cut the gold cleanly without damaging the cushion. Any slight nick in the blade will tear rather than cut the gold.

A gilder's tip Tips are brushes that are made by sandwiching a thin layer of badger hair between two pieces of card. They are available in different lengths. Generally for ceramic repairs the shortest length tip is the most useful. Tips can be cut into narrow lengths. Smaller tips (length and width) make it easier to handle the small quantities of gold leaf. Tips should be stored so that the hairs do not become bent. It is a good idea to store them between two pieces of stiff card.

A selection of good quality sable or squirrel brushes and liners as well as flat camel hair brushes will also be needed.

Figure 20. Gilding equipment showing:

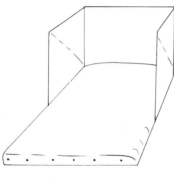

a A gilder's cushion

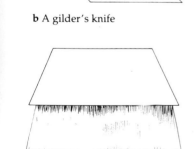

b A gilder's knife

c A gilder's tip

Applying gold leaf Gold leaf is not as easy to use as the other gilding materials described in this section but with practice and care the techniques can be mastered.

1 Mask surrounding areas but beware of applying adhesive tape to gilded surfaces; clingfilm is a better solution.

2 Before applying the size, lightly dust the area with talc, which prevents gold adhering to the surrounding area.

3 Apply size with a sable brush and wait for it to dry to a 'tacky' consistency.

4 To apply loose gold, cut it on a gilder's cushion into suitable sections with a gilder's knife, lift with a gilder's tip and lay it on the sized area. If you can do this without the gold dropping off the tip, or a draught of air whisking it off, you are doing well!

5 When using transfer gold, the design required can be traced gently onto the back of the tissue with a soft pencil or using carbon paper; cut to the appropriate shape and apply to the sized area. The transfer leaf can be gently rubbed with a small cotton wool pad to help it adhere. Use 100% cotton wool – viscose can scratch the gold. Dust off any excess leaf with a soft paint brush.

Hints

• *At the same time as applying the size to the repaired object a little should be applied to a ceramic tile. The size on the tile can then be tested for onset of tack (i.e. readiness to gild) with the tip of your finger. This prevents having to disturb and possibly disrupt the size on your object.*

• *Very fine abrasives such as the range supplied by Micromesh are excellent for finishing work (except on gold leaf).*

Lustres

A metallic finish or iridescent surface decoration on a ceramic body is known as 'lustre'. A lustre finish is perhaps the most difficult finish to replicate successfully and, as with all other techniques described in this book, will not be mastered without many trials and much error.

There are some commercially available media which are suitable for retouching. Liquitex have a range of acrylic paints with iridescent or metallic finishes. Daler-Rowney also produce a range of 'pearlescent' acrylic paints. Both manufacturers produce a range of colours, but it is unlikely that a correct colour match will be found without admixing. Acrylic colours or lustre powders are suitable for this purpose.

Lustre powders (e.g. Pearlescent, Hi-lite, Glimmer), bronze or metal powders (when mixed with a suitable binding medium), will also produce a metallic finish. Acrylic binding media, either water- or solvent-based, are the preferential binding media for lustre pigments. (Rustins Plastic Coating is another possible alternative, although not recommended because of the health and safety considerations.)

Techniques for simulating lustreware
Copper and bronze lustre When finishing a fill or moulding on an object to be coated in a lustre, abrade the repair down to a slightly lower level than the surrounding body, in order to allow for the several coats necessary for a satisfactory combination of colour, tone and iridescence. The first coat over an untinted fill should match the ground colour of the object.

Lustre may be applied by hand- or airbrush. Stir the mixture frequently; metallic particles are heavy and will sink to the bottom of a suspension. The area surrounding the fill should be masked off with clingfilm.

A dark bronze lustre finish can be achieved by adding burnt umber and indian red (mars red) to a suitable binding medium. Apply two to three coats, then mix dark bronze powder into the same mixture and apply on top of the previously applied paint. Abrade each layer with fine Micro-mesh cloths, and finish with a layer of clear varnish, polishing this last layer if necessary.

Other metallic finishes can be replicated in the same way as described above using the appropriate ground colours and metallic powders. A white ceramic tile is a good surface on which to practise.

Purple and pink (Sunderland) lustre Alizarin red and ultramarine blue will give a ground colour. The lustrous quality can be produced by adding powders from one of the 'hi-light' ranges, violet, pink or red as necessary.

Generally only one coat of pink lustre need be applied. Mix on a tile and practise a few brush strokes to achieve the desired effect. A sponged effect can be copied by using small pieces of natural sponge and dipping them into the premixed palette. Only when satisfied that the finish is the one which you require should you apply to the repair.

7 Four case studies

I An earthenware horse

Description
Staffordshire flat-back earthenware horse with two riders. Figure inscribed 'Returning Home'. The object was broken into two pieces, and the shard which should have fitted between the two pieces was missing. There was a lot of unidentified adhesive on the break edges.

Treatment plan
1 Clean, remove old adhesive
2 Replace missing part
3 Rebond
4 Fill in cracks and chips
5 Retouch/reglaze

Cleaning
The adhesive was thought to be animal glue because it was very thick and dark brown. The object was soaked in warm water and after about ten minutes the old adhesive began to soften and was gradually removed using a scalpel and stencil brush. When all traces of the adhesive had been removed the object was washed in Synperonic NBD detergent, rinsed and left for two weeks to dry out.

Replacing the missing part
Firstly a dental wax support was inserted behind the gap, which was then filled with Polyfilla mixed with a small amount of Evo-stick adhesive. The Polyfilla was shaped as much as possible while still soft and when the fill had hardened completely the pink dental wax support was removed. The fill was then trimmed along the break edge until the two pieces fitted together.

Rebonding
The break edges were de-greased with acetone. Paraloid B-72 was used to adhere the two pieces together. Elastic bands were used to keep the two pieces tightly clamped until the Paraloid had set completely.

Filling in
Fine Surface Polyfilla was used to fill in the small cracks and chips. This was abraded to a smooth surface with 3M Tri-m-ite abrasive papers (Grit 600 and 1000).

Retouching
Burnt sienna and unbleached titanium acrylic colours were sprayed on to retouch the repaired area on the body of the horse. The mane was coloured by hand using mars black acrylic paint. The retouched area was then lightly reglazed with one coat of Liquitex acrylic varnish that had been mixed with approximately 20% water to reduce the gloss to a satin finish.

See overleaf.

Four case studies

I An earthenware horse

Broken Staffordshire horse

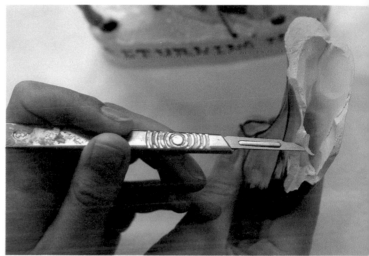

Dental wax support for plaster fill

Checking the wax support for a correct fit

The finished object

II A porcelain plate

Description
Minton raised paste, gilded plate (mark denotes plate was made between 1902 and 1911). Hard-paste porcelain.

The plate had been previously restored and the paint had yellowed. The restored gilding did not match the original.

Treatment plan
1 Dismantle previous restoration
2 Rebond
3 Fill in missing areas with coloured epoxy fill
4 Regild

Dismantling previous restoration
After several swab tests, it was found necessary to remove the previous restoration using Nitromors paint stripper. When the plate had been dismantled, more Nitromors was applied to the break edges to further soften the adhesive which was then completely removed using a scalpel and small toothbrush. The plate was then washed in Synperonic NBD and left to dry.

Bonding and filling
The break edges were de-greased with acetone and the plate, which was in four pieces, was rebonded by the dry stick method using Araldite 20/20. The adhesive tape was removed by soaking off in water to avoid damaging the gilding.

The white areas, which were very translucent, were filled with Araldite 20/20 bulked with fumed silica and coloured with minute quantities of zinc white, yellow ochre, raw umber and ultramarine blue powder pigments. When dry the areas were abraded to a fine, smooth and glossy finish with 3M Tri-m-ite abrasive papers, and finished with Micro-mesh cloths.

The design was retouched where necessary using Araldite 20/20 as a binding agent and powder pigments. When dry these areas were polished with Micro-mesh cloths. The ungilded areas were polished with Greygate plastic polish.

Regilding

Araldite 20/20 was mixed with a small amount of fumed silica and left to stand until slightly tacky; it was fluid enough to flow from a cocktail stick but not so runny that it did not stay in place (timing here was absolutely critical and many, many trials were undertaken before the correct viscosity was achieved). The Araldite 20/20 and fumed silica mixture was then applied with the point of a cocktail stick, following and reproducing the (raised paste) missing areas. This was carried out very slowly in several stages with the aid of a magnifying glass.

When dry the applied 'raised paste' was trimmed as necessary with the point of a sharp scalpel blade. After some three hours' work over several days, these areas were ready to be regilded.

The local area was dusted with a little talc from a no. 7 squirrel brush and painted over with Japan gold size. A tile was also painted with several small patches of Japan gold size, which were used to test for onset of tack. $23^{1}/_{4}$ carat Specially Selected gold leaf was cut to size and applied over the previously sized areas and then left for twenty-four hours to dry. The excess gold leaf was very gently removed with a small sable brush and the newly gilded areas gently polished with a small pad of cotton wool.

See overleaf.

II A Porcelain plate

Minton plate with old, discoloured repair

(right) Old repair coated with Nitromors to remove adhesive and paint

(opposite above) Taping the clean shards together for rebonding

(opposite below) Matching the gold leaf

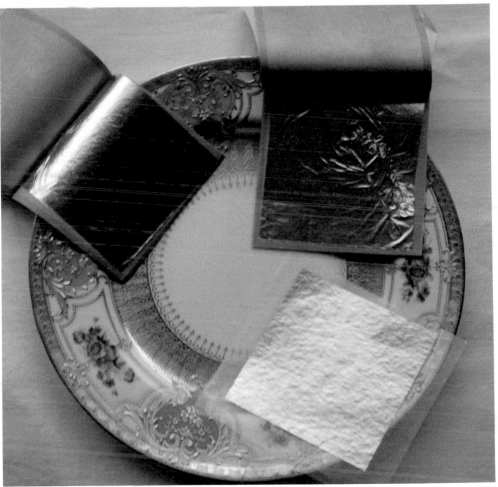

III A bone china coffee cup

Description
An unmarked (but signed F-Christie) bone china coffee cup with over-glaze enamel decoration on the outside. The inside of the cup and handle were gilded.

The cup had broken into two pieces, with two small V-shaped wedges missing. The object had not been previously repaired and was clean.

Treatment plan
1 Wash
2 Rebond
3 Cast missing pieces using dental wax mould
4 Retouch/Regild

Washing
The cup was washed in Synperonic NBD solution, rinsed and left to dry.

Rebonding
The break edges were de-greased with acetone and the cup was dry-stuck with Araldite 20/20 using magic tape to hold the pieces together. Excess adhesive was removed with an acetone swab before fully set. The cup was then left for twenty-four hours, after which time the magic tape was removed.

Making the missing parts
Pink dental wax sheets were cut to size and impressions taken from an intact edge. These small wax impressions were moved around to the areas to be cast and fixed in position using magic tape. A solution of Araldite 20/20 with titanium dioxide powder pigment was poured into the wax moulds. This was then left for twenty-four hours until the Araldite had set hard. The

dental wax and tape were removed, and the residue was cleaned off with an acetone swab and scalpel. The resulting cast was trimmed with a sharp scalpel and smoothed with abrasive papers.

Retouching and regilding

The missing design was repainted using Araldite 20/20 as a binding agent. This was mixed with raw sienna and chrome oxide green powder pigments to obtain a correct background match to the repaired areas. The design was painted in using the above pigments, lemon yellow and a little zinc white and terre verte. The areas worked on were abraded with Micro-mesh and retouched where necessary, being further abraded after each application of 20/20. Several tests were made to obtain the correct match to the interior gilding. No good colour match was found in gold leaf, so Schlag 2 metal leaf was used instead. The areas were then dusted with talc and the Schlag applied over a base of Japan gold size. When dry the Schlag was overpainted with Rowney acrylic gloss varnish tinted with a minute quantity of raw umber and alizarin crimson powder pigment.

When the varnish was completely dry (twenty-four hours) it was very gently abraded with a 12000 grit Micro-Mesh cloth. The outside of the cup was then polished with Renaissance wax.

See overleaf.

III A bone china coffee cup

Dental wax applied to an intact
edge

Dental wax mould moved
round to cover gap and taped
in place

Filled edge ready for retouching

Retouching the filled edge

IV A month in the life of a blue and white pot

The following case study illustrates how one object can require a variety of different processes.

Description

The pot when received was very fragile and dirty. Many of the rivets which had been embedded in plaster were very loose, and some had fallen out. About 80% of the break edges of the pot appeared to have no adhesive. One of the smaller shards had fallen out, and we decided to apply magic tape immediately to the more unstable areas of the pot, allowing a more detailed examination without the danger of the pot falling apart during handling.

The pot, measuring approximately 100 cm (40 in.) in height and 50 cm (20 in.) in diameter, was a white Chinese hard-paste porcelain pot decorated in under-glaze blue. There were a few small areas missing that were either unfilled or had been filled with a plaster type material. These areas of infill together with most of the rivet holes seemed to have suffered from shrinkage, causing the general unstable condition of the pot. There were rust stains around some of the rivets. The lid (approximately 20 cm / 8¼ in. in diameter) was in good condition apart from a large missing piece.

Despite the fact that the rivets belonged to the history of the piece, we decided to remove them as they were unsightly, very unstable and causing iron staining to the ceramic body.

Treatment plan

1 Remove rivets and dismantle pot
2 Clean and remove staining on pot and lid
3 Fill rivet holes with coloured fill
4 Assemble pot
5 Fill in missing areas with coloured fill
6 Make missing part of lid
7 Retouch/reglaze lid
8 Polish pot and lid

Day 1 – a.m.

The top of the pot was dismantled and the rivets removed just by gently pulling out by hand. The rivets at the bottom of the pot were more difficult to remove, but after soaking in warm water they came out easily.

The shards were first washed under running water with Synperonic NBD solution and rubbed with a small brush to remove the surface dirt. The pieces were then put into a bucket of Synperonic NBD solution with warm water and left to soak.
Time taken – 1½ hours

After an hour the pieces were removed, the rivet holes were cleaned out with a brush and scalpel blade, rinsed and dried, and Jenolite was applied to areas of iron staining.
Time taken – 1½ hours

Day 1 – p.m.

The progress of the Jenolite was checked periodically and it was removed after about an hour. The pieces were then washed and left to soak in detergent solution to remove staining and ingrained dirt.

The lid was washed and left to soak in Synperonic NBD solution to clean a crack.

Days 2–10

The pieces were checked periodically and the clean pieces removed from the detergent solution. These were then rinsed under running water and left to soak in clean water for two to three days, rinsed and left to dry. The remaining pieces were rinsed and returned to a new detergent solution. As the pieces began to dry out two of the shards were noted to have running cracks, and these cracks were sealed with Araldite 20/20 as soon as the pieces were dry.

Progress of lid cleansing was monitored and progressively harsher cleaning materials were employed to try to remove the dirt from the crack, culminating in the application of hydrogen peroxide swabs (60 volume undiluted).

Day 11

All pieces except two were now clean and most were dry or drying. The two remaining pieces were rinsed, dried with a soft cloth and then Jenolite was re-applied where necessary.

The Jenolite was removed after an hour and the pieces were washed and returned to soak in clean water. These two remaining pot shards were still not cleaned satisfactorily, and we decided to continue their cleaning with peroxide swabs. The shards were washed thoroughly under running water and left to soak overnight in clean water. After this peroxide swabs were applied to the areas to be treated. Progress was monitored and the swabs were removed after twenty-four hours, the pieces were washed, soaked and dried.

Days 12–14

The rivet holes were wiped over with an acetone swab and then filled with Araldite 20/20 which had been tinted to match the ground colour of the pot. Fumed silica and a little talc were used as bulking agents, and the Araldite 20/20 was tinted with the

following pigments: titanium white, ultramarine blue, raw umber, yellow ochre, terre verte. The final compound matched both the ground colour and opacity of the pot. The rivet holes were filled with this epoxy/bulking agent mixture to no more than two thirds of their capacity.

The lid appeared satisfactorily clean after about a week of treatment with peroxide swabs and was washed, soaked and rinsed and left to dry.

Day 15

A new batch of Araldite 20/20 filler was made up using ultramarine and raw umber to tint it, a small amount of fumed silica was added to obtain the correct translucency, and this was then used to finish filling the holes in the matching blue areas of the pot.

The crack in the lid was sealed with Araldite 20/20.

Day 16

Tests were carried out on the lid with various impression compounds to determine which would give the most satisfactory results for replacing the missing part of the lid. Pink dental wax was tried but was found not to give a detailed enough definition of the inside. Steramould worked better and was chosen as the appropriate material. Crystacal R was chosen as a casting medium because of the large size of the replacement part and the need for that part to be opaque.

Day 20

All the shards were now clean and dry, and most of the rivet holes had been very carefully filled, except for those that were on the break edges. The pot was then laid out in

IV A month in the life of a blue and white pot

Blue and white pot
showing old riveted repair
and broken lid

The old repair – rusting
metal rivets

Assembling and taping the clean shards

(right) Lid with replacement part ready for retouching

jigsaw fashion and assembled using magic tape to hold the shards together. The pot was first assembled in two parts: (i) from the base upwards, (ii) from the rim downwards (simply because this seemed to be the easiest way). The two parts were then assembled and left to stand securely on the work bench overnight.

Three unsuccessful casts were attempted on the lid, a fourth cast was successfully made. This was then abraded to a smooth surface suitable for retouching.

Day 21

The pot was rechecked to ensure that all the shards fitted together well and that there was no misalignment. After some minor adjustments the pot was deemed satisfactory except for one piece which seemed to have sprung. Tape and elastic bands were used to pull the edges more into alignment which slightly improved the situation, although after a considerable amount of time spent fiddling around it was decided that no further improvement could be made and the pot was now ready to be rebonded.

A solution of Araldite 20/20 was mixed and applied along the break lines using a cocktail stick. Excess adhesive was carefully wiped away after approximately two hours.

Days 22–24

Tape and excess adhesive having been removed, the gaps and holes were very carefully filled using Araldite 20/20 mixed with bulking and tinting agents (see Days 12–14). Magic tape was used as a support where necessary. When dry the Araldite fills were abraded with flour paper and then with Micro-mesh cloths.

A mix of acrylic paint was prepared for the lid, containing the palette: titanium white; ultramarine blue; yellow ochre; terre verte; raw umber. Two coats were sprayed by airbrush onto the plaster area. Liquitex acrylic airbrush medium was used to ensure that the paint was sufficiently dilute to be sprayed on smoothly. The inside of the lid was also sprayed with the above colours, and then part of that area was resprayed with a mixture of titanium white, raw umber and burnt sienna to blend in appropriately.

Day 25

The painted area of the lid was lightly abraded with an 8000 grit Micro-mesh cloth. The decorative details were then traced from an adjacent area and lightly drawn into position on the repaired area. These were then painted by hand, using an acrylic palette of ultramarine blue, alizarin crimson and raw umber. A selection of Winsor and Newton Sceptre gold brushes ranging from no. 1 spotter to a half-inch flat were used.

Day 26

The repaired area of the lid was finally sprayed with two coats of Rowney acrylic liquid gloss varnish.

No further finishing was required.

Day 30

The finished pot was cleaned of any sticky residue and finger marks using acetone swabs, and polished using Greygate plastic polish.

Glossary of materials

The following list contains some of the most common materials used in ceramic repair and mentioned in this book. Equivalent American product names are given in square brackets where appropriate.

Many of these products are hazardous to health and the environment. The hazard warnings indicate the degree of danger, but it is essential to read the full manufacturer's instructions regarding use, storage and disposal before use. If instructed not to breathe fumes, ensure that the room is well ventilated or use an extraction hood; in the case of dust or particles, wear a dust mask. Wear disposable gloves (or household rubber gloves for the less powerful products such as detergents) if instructed to avoid skin contact.

Acetone (2-propanone; dimethylketone) A highly flammable solvent used to dilute **Paraloid B-72** and cellulose nitrate adhesives, as well as uncured epoxy resins. It will remove some acrylic paints and varnishes. It evaporates quickly and used sensibly is one of the least toxic solvents.

- *Highly flammable*
- *Do not inhale fumes*
- *Avoid skin contact*

Acrylic paint Plastic acrylic resin suspended in water. A wide range of these products is available from various manufacturers (paints, varnishes, lustres and gold colours). Generally safe, easy to use and mostly water soluble.

Ambersil Silicone rubber moulding compound. Mixing amounts are critical – consult manufacturer's instructions.

Ammonia solution (ammonium hydroxide solution NH_4OH). A pungent smelling solution made by dissolving ammonia gas in water. It can cause burns and is irritating to skin, eyes and respiratory system. Pressure may develop in the bottle – open with care. To use – add a few drops to hydrogen peroxide solution when removing stains from high-fired wares.

- *Harmful, use with caution*
- *Do not inhale fumes*
- *Avoid skin contact*

Araldite adhesives Several different types of epoxy resin adhesives are available with this name. All are a combination of resin and hardener, in varying mix ratios (referred to in this text as two-part epoxies).

- *All epoxy hardeners are irritants and toxic*
- *Avoid skin contact*
- *Do not inhale fumes*

Araldite 20/20 A clear, low viscosity type. Mix ratio is 3:1 by volume. Sets in 24 hours at 20°C (68°F).
Araldite AY103/HY956 A clear, moderately low viscosity type. Mix ratio by volume 100 resin: 18/20 parts hardener. Sets in 24 hours at 20°C (68°F).
Araldite Epoxy A slightly yellow-brown high viscosity adhesive. Mix equal parts, sets in 12 hours.
Araldite Rapide A slightly yellow-brown, high viscosity, fast setting adhesive. Mix equal parts, sets in 5 minutes at 20°C (68°F).

Ariel [Tide] This proprietary washing powder is useful for surface stain removal on glazed earthenwares and non-porous materials. Use approximately one tablespoon in a litre (approx. 2 pt) of water for a cleaning solution.
• *Avoid skin contact with concentrated solutions*

Barytes (barium sulphate) A white pigment and bulking material. Useful in epoxy fills.
• *Do not inhale dust*

Biotex A proprietary brand of biological washing powder containing certain enzymes which catalyze the breakdown of proteins. Useful as a stain remover. Use one tablespoon to a litre (2 pt) of water.
• *Avoid skin contact with concentrated solutions*

Bronze powders Finely powdered metal particles used to simulate gold and bronze lustres on ceramics. Mix with an appropriate varnish or paint medium.
• *Do not inhale dust*

Calgon (sodium hexametaphosphate) A proprietary water softener used in conjunction with **Biotex** or any other biological detergent to remove stains from porcelains. Use one tablespoon to a litre (2 pt) of water. Lustres and gilding may be affected.
• *Avoid skin contact with concentrated solutions*

Cellulose nitrate A high viscosity adhesive commonly used in ceramic repair, diluted with acetone. Common brand name is HMG.
• *Highly flammable*
• *Vapour harmful in confined spaces*

Crystacal R A plaster product with a high alpha content – see **Plaster**.

Cyanoacrylates Instant glues – see **Superglue**.

Dental wax sheets Pink sheets (20 cm × 7 cm – 8 in. × 2¾ in.) of wax used as a moulding material, easily softened in warm water or with a hair dryer

Devcon 5-minute Epoxy A high viscosity epoxy adhesive similar to Araldite Rapide.
• *Irritant, avoid skin contact*
• *Do not inhale fumes*

Devcon Magicbond An epoxy putty supplied in a single tube. The roll consists of two colours, which when cut to size and mixed become a one-colour, white modelling putty. It sets hard in an hour.
• *Irritant*
• *Avoid skin contact*
• *Do not inhale dust*

Dichloromethane – See **Nitromors**.

Epoxy resin adhesives Two-part adhesives consisting of varying ratios of resin and hardener which set by chemical reaction. Used for porcelain and stoneware repairs. Most hardeners can cause skin irritation or dermatitis. See **Araldite**, **Devcon**, **Fynebond**, **HXTAL NYL-1** and **UHU 300+**.

- *All epoxy hardeners are irritants and toxic*
- *Avoid skin contact*
- *Do not inhale fumes*

Fumed silica Very finely powdered silica used as a matting agent in paints and varnishes. Also as a bulking agent for epoxy resin fills.

- *Do not inhale dust*

Fynebond Low viscosity epoxy adhesive.

- *Irritant*

Gold leaf Real gold, in sheets of 80 mm × 80 mm (3 in. × 3 in.) available either loose leaf or backed on tissue (transfer gold), in various colours or carats. Apply onto gold size. Requires some special equipment – knife, gilder's pad and tips.

Gold size An oil based medium with 'tack times' varying from 1 to 24 hours, depending on air temperature. Clean brushes with white spirit.

Gold colours Oil based varnishes (various types available) with bronze powders mixed in. Differing types have either white spirit or xylene as solvent; avoid the latter.

Gold lacquers Often **shellac** based products with bronze powders, these may be suitable for small areas but tarnishing may be a problem. Use industrial methylated spirits as a solvent.

Gold paints Acrylic gold coloured paint is reasonably good for small areas, inexpensive, usually safe and easy to use. Clean brushes in water.

Greygate plastic polish Used as a final polish for epoxy resin fills. Apply polish, leave to dry and rub off with soft cloth.

- *Flammable*

Hydrogen peroxide (H_2O_2) A bleaching agent (and disinfectant) which gives off oxygen so do not store with flammable solvents (because of fire risk). Available in volume strengths, apply onto cotton wool swabs over discoloured cracks, activate with a few drops of **Ammonia solution**. Do not use on dry ceramics.

- *Avoid skin contact*

HXTAL NYL-1 A water-white, two-part, low viscosity epoxy adhesive, developed especially for conservation purposes. Excellent for dry-sticking glass and porcelain. Expensive, requires specific mixing in proportions of 100 resin: 30 hardener. May discolour if in contact with **hydrogen peroxide** residue and some other adhesives.

- *Irritant*

ICI Autocolour Also known as Belco, this is a cellulose stopper commonly used as a car body filler. May be used as a paint-on filler for thread cracks in high-fired wares. Dilute with cellulose thinners if a less viscous substance is required. Caution: contains xylene, lead and harmful isomers.

- *Harmful and flammable*
- *Avoid skin contact*
- *Do not inhale vapour*

Jenolite A phosphoric acid based rust remover. Use sparingly to remove iron staining from ceramics; can react with iron compounds in low fired ceramics.

- *Corrosive*
- *Avoid skin contact*

Kaolin (china clay or hydrated aluminium silicate) Used in porcelain production; may be used as a bulking agent with epoxy adhesives (but talc is a better option).

- *Do not inhale dust*

Laponite A synthetic inorganic colloid powder, which forms a thick gel when mixed with water; use as a poultice to remove ingrained stains. May be mixed with some solvents, e.g. white spirit or cleaning agents (**hydrogen peroxide**).

- *Irritant*
- *Do not inhale dust*

Maimeri Restoration colours These top quality paints are finely ground pigments bound in mastic (a tree resin), which are soluble in white spirit; they can be mixed with solvent based acrylic varnish or applied and then coated with a gloss varnish.

Marble powder Finely powdered marble available in different 'grit' sizes, used as a bulking agent with epoxy adhesive for fills on porcelain, especially Parian.

- *Do not inhale dust*

Masking tape For masking off areas; do not apply over gilding or unfired decoration. As with any tape do not leave on surface for longer than necessary.

Melinex [Mylar] Transparent polyester film useful for mixing adhesives and retouching media.

Microballoons Inert fine hollow glass beads, used as a bulking agent.

Micro-mesh An excellent range of extra fine abrasives. Available in cloth form or mounted on flexi files (available from some cosmetic retailers as nail files).

Milliput A two-part epoxy putty. Use equal amounts and mix thoroughly. An easy-to-use filler and modelling material, sets hard in 24 hours.

- *May irritate skin*

Nitromors [Zylonyte] (dichloromethane and methanol) A powerful degreaser, paint remover and epoxy adhesive softener; available as water soluble (green label) or spirit soluble (yellow label). Water soluble is preferable for ceramic restoration use. This is potentially the most hazardous material used in ceramic repair and should be used in a well ventilated area, preferably in a fume hood or with air extraction.

- *Harmful, avoid skin contact*
- *Do not inhale fumes*

Paraloid B-72 [Acryloid B-72] (ethylmethacrylate copolymer) A conservation 'approved' adhesive, available as granules but more usefully in tubes dissolved in **acetone**. A close rival of **cellulose nitrate** adhesive. Easy to use, reversible in acetone. Useful for consolidation and all sorts of ceramic repair, particularly earthenwares.

- *Highly flammable*

Plaster products (hydrated calcium sulphate) Commercial varieties have a cellulose base. Always add plaster to water (3:1) to prevent lumps forming. Some types e.g. **Crystacal R** are particularly dense and hard, and therefore more suitable for opaque porcelain and stoneware. **Polyfilla** [US Polycell] is widely available. **Fine Surface Polyfilla** is ready mixed and is used for fine cracks and gaps only.

- *Do not inhale dust when mixing or sanding*

Polyester pastes Styrene based pastes generally used as car body fillers. Common examples are Isopon P38 [Upol] and F.E.W. Mix with hardener (dibenzoylperoxide) to activate paste. For use on porcelain (opaque) and stoneware, for filling in small chips.

- *Irritant*
- *Flammable*
- *Do not breathe fumes*

PVA [White Neutral ph] Polyvinyl acetate adhesive, commonly known as white wood glue or Evo-stick woodworking adhesive. Can be used to stick earthenwares or as a strengthener for plaster mixes. It may also be mixed with powder pigments to produce a surface coating. Soluble in water or acetone when set.

- *May irritate skin*

Renaissance wax Micro-crystalline wax polish for ceramics, furniture etc. Do not use over repaired areas where acrylic products have been used.

Rhoplex AC-33 An acrylic dispersion adhesive for use on low-fired wares. Common in the USA.

- *May irritate skin*

Rubber latex A vulcanised natural rubber impression material (contains ammonia which may react with metals especially copper). Shrinks quickly; remove once set.

- *Do not inhale fumes*
- *Avoid skin contact*

Rustins Plastic Coating Plastic coating which is a mixture of butylated urea formaldehyde, melamine and alkyd resins in a solvent of aromatic hydrocarbons and alcohols. The hardener is a mixture of inorganic acid and alcohol. Used as a surface coating to simulate glaze, can be tinted using **Maimeri** Restoration powder pigments. Until recently very popular with many ceramic restorers, but losing popularity due to toxicity and availability of other less hazardous products, e.g. acrylics.

- *Harmful, avoid skin contact*
- *Do not inhale fumes*

Schlag metal leaf A variety of metal leaf used for gilding purposes where gold leaf will not produce a good colour match.

Scotch magic tape The most suitable type of adhesive tape – more easily removed than Sellotape or ordinary Scotch tape, which are common alternatives, but not as gentle. Use with a dispenser for ease of use. Avoid leaving any adhesive tape on ceramics for prolonged periods of time.

Sepiolite A white clay product used as a poulticing material.

- *Do not inhale dust*

Shellac A sticky resin produced by the lac beetle and dissolved in industrial methylated spirit. Sometimes known as

French polish, it has been used as an adhesive in the past, and also as a sealant on plaster. Not recommended.

Silicone rubber A catalyst-activated siliconized rubber solution. Care should be taken when mixing to avoid air bubbles being trapped. A dusting of talc on the surface of the area to be moulded helps to prevent the mixture adhering to the surface. Will stain porous earthenware.

- *Do not inhale fumes*
- *Avoid skin contact*

Steramould A two-part silicone moulding compound, safe and easy to use (developed for taking impressions of human ears for hearing aids). May stain unglazed earthenwares.

Superglue A popular name for **cyanoacrylate adhesives**. Advertized as a wonderful 'cure-all' for any broken object. In fact generally quite unsuitable for ceramic restoration purposes. May be useful for holding pieces together before 'dry sticking'. Difficult to break down; superglue remover (**acetone** or **Nitromors**) may be used. Use with caution only on high-fired wares if absolutely necessary.

- *Do not inhale fumes*
- *Avoid skin contact*

Synperonic NBD A non-ionic liquid detergent for general cleaning purposes.

- *Irritant*

Synthetic onyx powder A fine granular powder. Useful as a bulking agent for mixing with epoxy adhesives to create fills for porcelain and Parian wares.

- *Do not inhale dust*

Talc (magnesium sulphate) Sometimes called French chalk, it is a useful bulking agent for epoxy fills and as a release agent when applying moulding material or to prevent gold leaf sticking to surfaces. Dust on with small paint brush.

- *Do not inhale dust*

Titanium dioxide An opaque, brilliant white pigment for tinting, painting and bulking epoxy resin fills.

- *Do not inhale dust*

Tri-m-ite Waterproof silicon carbide sandpaper, manufactured by 3M. May be used wet or dry, available in 4 grit sizes, P280–P1000.

UHU 300+ A two-part high viscosity epoxy adhesive, consisting of equal parts of resin and hardener. Dries in 12 hours at 20°C (68°F). Slightly brownish, but small quantities of white pigment can be added to enable it to be used on stoneware and porcelain.

- *Irritant, avoid skin contact*

Zinc oxide A commonly used white pigment for painting, bulking and tinting. Not as intensely white as **titanium dioxide**.

- *Do not inhale dust*

Manufacturers and suppliers in the UK

Many of the materials recommended in this book can be purchased from general DIY or hardware stores or good artists' supply shops. There are also a number of general craft suppliers which stock a wide range of restoration materials, as well as specialist suppliers of specific products. Where materials cannot be purchased directly, ask the manufacturer for details of your nearest stockist.

General conservation and art specialists

Arcesso
194 Blue House Lane
Oxted
Surrey RH8 ODE
Tel: 01883 73034

Conservation Resources
Unit 1
Pony Road
Horspath Industrial Estate
Cowley
Oxford OX4 2RD
Tel: 01865 747755

Stuart Stevenson
68 Clerkenwell Road
London EC1M 5QA
Tel: 0171 253 1693

Adhesives

General conservation and art specialists

Araldite, superglue and PVAs
DIY or hardware stores

Araldite 20/20
CIBA-Geigy Polymers
Duxford
Cambridge CB3 4QA
Tel: 01223 832121

Devcon adhesives
Devcon UK
Brunel Close
Park Farm
Wellingborough
Northants
Tel: 01933 675299

Fynebond
Fyne Conservation Services
Airds Cottage
St. Catherines
by Loch Fyne
Argyle PA25 8BA
Tel: 01369 860388

Paraloid B72, cellulose nitrate
H. Marcel Guest Ltd
Riverside Works
Collyhurst Road
Manchester M40 7RU
Tel: 0161 205 7631

Books (including out-of-print titles)

Archetype Books
31–34 Gordon Square
London WC1H 0PY
Tel: 0171 387 9651

Reference Works
12 Commercial Road
Swanage
Dorset BH19 1DF
Tel: 01929 424423

HMSO Publications
HSE Information Centre
Broad Lane
Sheffield S3 7HQ
Tel: 01742 892345

Brushes and airbrushes

Artists' supply shops or

CLE Design Ltd
69–71 Haydens Road
Wimbledon
London SW19 111Q
Tel: 0181 540 5772

Airbrush & Spray Centre
39 Littlehampton Road
Worthing
West Sussex BN13 1QJ
Tel: 01903 266991

Cleaning products

Proprietary detergents and water softeners
Supermarkets or hardware stores

Nitromors paint stripper, poultice materials, Synperonic NBD and general chemical cleaners
DIY or hardware stores or

P Merck Ltd
Hunter Boulevard
Magna Park
Lutterworth
Leics LE17 9XN
Tel: 01455 558 600

Griffin & George
Bishop Meadow Road
Loughborough
Leics LE11 0RG
Tel: 01509 233344

Acetone, hydrogen peroxide
Hairdresser supply shops or chemist shops

Steam cleaners
John Quayle Dental
Manufacturing Co. Ltd
Derotor House
Dominion Way
Worthing
West Sussex BN14 8QN
Tel: 01903 204427

Filling, modelling and moulding materials

General conservation
and art specialists

Ambersil (silicone rubber)
Ambersil
Wylds Road
Castlefield Ind. Est.
Bridgwater
Somerset TA6 4DD
Tel: 01278 424200

Dental wax
Cottrel & Co.
15 Charlotte Street
London W1P 2AA
Tel: 0171 580 5500

Devcon Magicbond
Devcon UK

Isopon P38, F.E.W.
Car accessory shops

Microballoons
GRP Factors
21st Avenue
Blue Bridge Industrial Estate
Halstead
Essex CO9 9EX
Tel: 01787 47230

Milliput
Unit 5
The Marian
Dolgellau
Gwynead
Mid Wales
Tel: 01341 422562

Polyfilla, Fine Surface Polyfilla
DIY or hardware stores

Steramould
A & M Hearing
Faraday Road
Crawley
Sussex
Tel: 01293 540471

Finishing materials

Greygate plastic polish
DIY or hardware stores

Micro-mesh abrasive systems
PW Products
2nd Floor
64–66 High Street
Barnet
Herts EN5 5SJ
Tel: 0181 441 4151

Renaissance wax
Quality DIY or hardware
stores or:
Renaissance Products Ltd
Picreator Enterprises Ltd
London NW4 2PN
Tel: 0181 202 8972

Tri-m-ite sandpaper
3M UK Plc
3M House – PO Box 1
Bracknell
Berks RG12 1JU
Tel: 01344 858000

Pigments and general art supplies

Powder pigments, Lefranc and Bourgeois and Rowney Cryla products
General conservation
and art specialists,
artists' supply shops, or

A P Fitzpatrick
1 Barnabas Studios
10–22 Barnabas Road
London E9 5SB
Tel: 0181 985 7865

L. Cornelissen & Son Ltd
105 Great Russell Street
London WC1B 3RY
Tel: 0171 636 1045

W Habberley Meadows Ltd
5 Saxon Way
Chelmsley Wood
Birmingham B37 5AY
Tel: 0121 770 0103

Liquitex artists' products
Artists' supply shops or

Liquitex
Binney & Smith (Europe) Ltd
Ampthill Road
Bedford MK42 9RS
Tel: 01234 360201

Gilding materials
Messrs E Ploton (Sundries)
273 Archway Road
London N6 5AA
Tel: 0181 348 0315

Glaze, Rustins plastic coating, varnish
Rustins Ltd
Waterloo Road
London NW2 7TX
Tel: 0181 450 4666

Maimeri products
Osborne & Butler Ltd
Osbourne House
Hoo Farm
Kidderminster DY11 7RA
Tel: 01562 515 269

Specialist conservation equipment

General conservation
and art specialists

General instruments
C.Z. Scientific
1 Elstree Way
Borehamwood
Herts WD6 1NH
Tel: 0181 953 1688

Lighting and air extraction equipment
CLE Design Ltd
69–71 Haydens Road
Wimbledon
London SW19 1IQ
Tel: 0181 540 5772

Safety equipment, respirators
James North & Son Ltd
PO Box 3
Market Street
Hyde, Cheshire SK14 1RL
Tel: 0161 368 5811

Small scales and instruments
Rubin & Son (UK) Ltd
83 Clerkenwell Road
Hatton Garden
London EC1 5AR
Tel: 0171 242 5880

Sentinel Laboratories Hcl
Mitchell House
The Mardens
Crawley
West Sussex RH11 0AQ
Tel: 01293 526457

Manufacturers and suppliers in the USA

Many of the materials recommended in this book can be purchased from general hardware stores or good graphic supply stores. There are also a number of general craft suppliers which stock a range of conservation materials, as well as specialist suppliers of specific products.

Only suppliers of products available in the USA have been listed here. If you require a product that is not available in the USA, consult a specialist supplier for a US equivalent or order from a foreign supplier (see UK list).

General conservation and art specialists

Conservation Materials Ltd
1165 Marietta Way
PO Box 2884
Sparks, NV 89431
Tel: 702 331 0582
Fax: 702 331 0588

Fisher Scientific
711 Forbes Avenue
Pittsburgh, PA 15219
Tel: 412 562 8300
Fax: 412 562 5344

Conservation Resources
International
800-H Forbes Place
Springfield, VA 22151
Tel: 703 321 7730
Fax: 703 321 0629

Adhesives

Acryloid B-72
Fisher Scientific

Rhoplex AC-33 and Araldite
CIBA-Geigy Co.
Formulated Systems Group
4917 Dawn Avenue
East Lansing, MI 48823
Tel: 517 351 5900
Fax: 517 351 9003

Devcon adhesives
The above suppliers or

Devcon Corp.
30 Endicott Street
Danvers, MA 01923
Tel: 508 777 1100
Fax: 508 774 0516

White neutral ph adhesives and supergluc
Hardware stores or lumber yards

UHU 300+
Manco Inc
830 Canterbury Road
Westlake, OH 44145-1462
Tel: 216 892 4505
Fax: 216 892 9256

Brushes and airbrushes

Graphic supply shops

Cleaning products

Proprietary detergents and water softeners
Supermarkets and hardware stores

Acetone and hydrogen peroxide
Hardware stores or pharmacists

Zynolyte paint remover, poultice materials, Synperonic NBD and general chemical cleaners
Hardware stores or
Conservation Material Ltd,
Conservation Resources
International, Fisher Scientific

Filling, modelling and moulding materials

General craft supplies, calcium sulphate (plaster of Paris) and other plaster
Conservation Materials Ltd,
Conservation Resources
International, Fisher Scientific

Milliput
Scientific Mod Inc.
340 Snyder Avenue
Berkley Heights, NJ 07922
Tel: 201 464 7070
Fax: 201 665 9393

Verlinden, Letterman & Stock
(Legacy Distributors)
Lone Star Industrial Park
811 Lone Star Drive
Ofallon, MO 63366
Tel: 314 281 5700
Fax: 314 281 5750

Devcon Magicbond
Devcon Corp.

UPOL (polyester paste)
Automotive wholesalers

Finishing materials

Micro-mesh abrading system
Micro-Surface Finishing
Products Inc.
Box 818
Wuton, IA 52778
Tel: 319 732 3240
Fax: 319 732 3390

Renaissance wax
Cutlery Specialities
22 Morris Lane
Great Neck, NY 11024
Tel: 516 829 5899
Fax: 516 773 8076

Tri-m-ite sandpaper
3M
3M Twin Cities Sales Center
PO Box 33211
St. Paul, MN 55133-3211
Tel: 612 733 3300
Fax: 612 736 1379

Pigments and general art supplies

Powder pigments, Lefranc and Bourgeois, Daler-Rowney and Maimeri products
Graphic supply shops or
Conservation Materials Ltd,
Conservation Resources
International

Liquitex
The above suppliers or

Binney & Smith Inc.
1100 Church Lane
PO Box 431
Eastern, PA 18144 0431

Specialist conservation equipment

General
Conservation Materials Ltd,
Conservation Resources
International,
Fisher Scientific

Small scales and instruments
Rubin & Son, USA Inc.
96 Spring Street
New York, NY 10012
Tel: 212 966 6300
Fax 212 966 6354

Conservation advice and further study

There are a number of advisory bodies and professional organisations in the field of conservation where information can be obtained on training and other matters relating to the conservation of ceramics.

In the UK

The United Kingdom
Institute for Conservation
(UKIC)
6 Whitehorse Mews
Westminster Bridge Road
London SE1 7QD
Tel: 0171 620 3371
(Publishers of *Conservation News* and headquarters of the Ceramic and Glass Conservation Group, which meets twice yearly)

The Conservation Unit
Museums and Galleries
Commission
16 Queen Anne's Gate
London SW1H 9AA
Tel: 0171 233 4200

Scottish Society for
Conservation and Restoration
The Glassite Meeting House
33 Barony Street
Edinburgh EH3 6NX
Tel: 0131 556 8417

Historic Scotland
Scottish Conservation Bureau
Longmore House
Salisbury Place
Edinburgh EH9 1SH
Tel: 0131 668 8668

In the USA

American Institute for
Conservation of Historic
and Artistic Works
1717 K Street NW, # 301
Washington DC 20006
Tel: 202 452 9545

In Ireland

Irish Professional
Conservators' and
Restorers' Organisation
c/o National Gallery
of Ireland
Merrion Square
Dublin 2
Ireland
Tel: 01-6615 133

Client-Conservator agreement

It is recommended that the conservator should enter into a simple form of agreement with the client on delivery of the broken object for repair, covering such items as the work to be carried out, the price, payment, insurance and non-collection of the object etc. An example of such an agreement which may be used is set out overleaf. However, the precise terms to be used are a matter of individual choice or negotiation with the client and the conservator may wish to adopt modified terms from those recommended. This example applies to English law.

No responsibility whatsoever is accepted by the authors or publishers of this book for this agreement and, in particular, as to whether it achieves its intended purposes. The conservator is advised to take his/her own legal advice before using these terms or any variations to them. It should particularly be noted that the courts have power to disallow certain types of terms in certain contracts deemed to be 'unfair' and it is possible that some of the terms set out on the following page could be challenged on these grounds.

Terms and conditions

A This agreement is made between the Conservator and the Client whose respective details appear in the particulars overleaf ('the Particulars').

B The work The Conservator will carry out the conservation/restoration work specified in the Particulars ('the work') to the object or objects therein specified ('the object'). Whilst the Conservator will endeavour to carry out the work with reasonable care and skill no responsibility to the Client is undertaken to that effect and the Conservator shall in no circumstances be liable to the Client for any damage to or loss or destruction of the object whether or not caused by the negligence of the Conservator or any other person and however caused.

C The price Where an estimate is given by the Conservator such estimate is open for acceptance by the Client for a period of two months failing which it may at the sole discretion of the Conservator be revised. The Conservator will endeavour to ensure that the final price chargeable to the Client is within the estimate (plus any agreed additional costs) but reserves the right to increase the price above the estimate where the work required proves to be greater and/or more time-consuming than originally anticipated.

D Payment Unless the contrary appears in the Particulars then payment of the final price notified to the Client by the Conservator is due from the Client upon collection of the conserved/restored object.

E Insurance The object remains at the entire risk of the Client. It is accordingly the Client's responsibility to insure the object in such sums and for such risks as the Client shall think fit and no such insurance shall be taken out by the Conservator.

F Cancellation Where the Conservator has commenced the work and this Agreement is cancelled by the Client prior to completion the Conservator shall in lieu of damages for breach of contract be entitled to require the payment of that part of the estimated price proportionate to the amount of the work carried out.

G Duration The Conservator will endeavour to complete the work with all due diligence but any dates given or periods of time quoted are estimates only and shall not be the ground for any claim for loss or compensation against the Conservator.

H Completion Unless the contrary appears in the Particulars the Conservator shall notify the Client of completion of the work by post or telephone to the address or telephone number for the Client noted in the Particulars. It is the Client's responsibility to notify any change of address or telephone number.

I Collection It shall be the obligation of the Client to collect the object after notification by the Conservator of the completion of the work. If the object is not collected within six months of the date of such notification then title to the object shall pass to the Conservator who shall be free to sell the same and from the net proceeds to recover such sums as may be due to the Conservator under this Agreement. The Conservator shall then hold the balance of such proceeds (if any) for the Client for a further period of twelve months after such sale but shall thereafter be entitled to retain the same for the Conservator's own benefit if not claimed by the Client by the end of that period.

J Copyright The Conservator retains the copyright in all reports drawings or photographs prepared under this Agreement which may not be reproduced in whole or in part without the Conservator's consent which may be given on terms or declined with or without reason.

K This Agreement is governed by the provisions of English law.

Name, address and telephone number of Conservator   Date

Name, address and telephone number of Client

Description of object

Agreed conservation/restoration work   The Conservator will notify
of completion by telephone

Estimated cost   £   + VAT

Additional costs Materials, carriage,
research, visits, photographs etc.   £   + VAT

Agreement
The Conservator agrees to repair the Object and the Client delivers it for repair subject
to the Terms and Conditions set out overleaf.

Signature of Client   **Date**   **Signature of Conservator**   **Date**

Suggested further reading

Pottery & Porcelain Bernard H Charles (David & Charles 1974)
An Illustrated Encyclopedia of British Pottery & Porcelain
Geoffrey Godden (Magna Books 1992)
The Dictionary of Minton Paul Atterbury & Maureen Batkin
(Antique Collectors' Club 1990)
Italian Maiolica Timothy Wilson (Phaidon 1989)
Worcester Porcelain Dinah Renolds (Ashmolean/Christies
Handbooks 1989)
Chinese Porcelain Anthony Du Boulay (Weidenfeld & Nicolson
1963)
Coalport & Coalbrookdale Porcelain Geoffrey Godden
(Herbert Jenkins 1970)
An Illustrated Dictionary of Ceramics G Savage and
H Newman (Thames & Hudson 1985)
Painting with Acrylics Jenny Rodwell (Macdonald 1986)
The Materials and Techniques of Painting Emma Pearce
(Jonathan Stephenson Thames & Hudson 1989)
Creative Airbrushing Graham Duckett (The Promotional
Reprint Company Ltd for Bookmart Ltd 1992)
Ceramic Masterpieces W David Kingery and Pamela
B Vandiver (Free Press 1986)
English Earthenware Figures Pat Halfpenny (Antique
Collectors Club 1991)
Looking at European Ceramics – A Guide to Technical Terms.
David Harris Cohen/Catherine Hess (Getty/BMP 1993)
English Polychrome Delftware and its Repair Dr J Black
(UKIC conservation paper 1993)
The Preservation of Delftware Tiles in British Architecture
Hans Van Lemmen (English Heritage conservation paper 1994)
Cleaning Agents – Considerations for Ceramic Conservators
Lorna R Green, British Museum (UKIC conservation paper
1992)
Pigments & Brushes Emma Pearce (UKIC Publication 1993)
Lighting Requirements for Conservators & Restorers John
Money (Paper to accompany CLE Design Ltd catalogue, 1993)